Dear Trainer...

Dealing with difficult problems in training

Sara Thorpe &
Jackie Clifford

KOGAN
PAGE

First published in 2000

Kogan Page Limited
120 Pentonville Road
London N1 9JN
UK

Stylus Publishing Inc.
22883 Quicksilver Drive
Sterling, VA 20166-2012
USA

© Jackie Clifford and Sara Thorpe, 2000

British Library Cataloguing in Publication Data

A CIP record for this book is available from the British Library.

ISBN 0 7494 3389 2

Typeset by Kogan Page
Printed and bound in Great Britain by Biddles Ltd, *www.biddles.co.uk*

Contents

Acknowledgements

Dear Reader,

This book is dedicated to all trainers everywhere, and especially to Geoff and Majid – our favourite trainers. And to Claire (Jackie's Mum) and George (Sara's Dad).

From
Jackie and Sara

Dear Reader:
Introduction

We hatched the idea for this book over dinner one evening. Two ex-colleagues meeting after several years, we found ourselves discussing how we missed working in a team with other trainers. Now, both working in more solitary surroundings, we realized the value of having a colleague on site to offer advice, support and a shoulder to cry on! By the time dessert had arrived, we had reminisced about good and bad times, and discussed how we might find the support we'd lost.

We came to the conclusion that whilst there are many excellent publications out there, containing vast amounts of information and theories about training, what we wanted was something that was easy to read, made practical suggestions and would be a substitute for discussing problems with another person. We wanted a 'mentor we could put in our pocket'! Even after many years' experience, we still felt the need for support, so we believed others would feel the same. That's why we wrote this book.

The aim of the book is to help new and experienced trainers alike. We are not setting ourselves up as experts who always get things right. We know that we are still learning, and that situations arise that we are unsure about. These might be new to us, or catch us unawares. But we also know that we have a lot of experience we can draw on when faced with the challenges of our chosen role. We simply want to share our experiences with you, and show you that you are not alone.

The book is written in the form of e-mails we have sent to each other, not mentor to mentee, trainer to trainee, but colleague to colleague, friend to friend. The individuals and places mentioned are fictional, in as much as we have changed names, sexes, and situations sufficiently to keep the identities of trainees and colleagues confidential.

Each communication is based on our experience of situations we have faced during our years as training professionals with various organizations. These situations include dealing with a participant who disrupted the course, and a manager who would not let any of her staff attend our training. Some we simply did not handle very well, others we coped with, but not as well as we felt we could have. For each e-mail there is a reply in which the respondent offers ideas on what could or could not have been done differently. In some cases there is a follow-up e-mail detailing what happened when any advice was actioned.

The e-mails are dated as if they were sent during the course of one year, but we must confess that all the situations described have not happened to us in the space of a year, but reflect our experiences sincewe began training over 10 years ago. We hope that in any year of your career, only a few of the things described in the e-mails happen to you!

How to use this book

When we wrote the book, it was our intention that you would dip in and out of it when you needed to, just as you would discuss a particular day's course with a colleague. For ease of use, the e-mails are arranged in subject rather than date order. We created the matrix of the problems and solutions covered in the e-mails so that you can easily find situations similar to those you are faced with, read the relevant e-mails and either be inspired with new ideas or feel reassured that you are going down the right track. Alternatively, just read the book from cover to cover; and share with us a very hectic year.

At the end of the book you will find a synopsis of each topic covered and useful tools such as a sample training needs analysis questionnaire and checklists covering many aspects of training. There is also a list of suggested further reading and a glossary of terms.

Regards
Jackie and Sara

Matrix of e-mail problems and solutions

	E-MAIL NUMBER		
TOPIC	PROBLEM	SOLUTIONS	ALSO SEE...
Clarifying training needs			
Handling disagreements	24	25, 26	
Identifying the real need	51	52–53	12, 29
Methods			53, 108–110
Presenting findings	54	55–56	
Designing interventions			
Working with others	1	2–3	
Taking a systematic approach	1	2–3	
Creativity	43, 46, 74	44–45, 47, 75	60–61
Selecting activities	60	61	
Using videos	105	106	
Length of courses	72	73	
Induction	84	85–86	
Outdoor training	87	88–90	
Residential courses	103	104	
Delivering training			
Administration	7	8–10	
Pre- and post-course work	64	65–66	
Learning styles			11–15, 42
Equal opportunities	62	63	
Confidentiality	70	71	5–6
Creativity	46	40–42	44–45, 47
Equipment failure	39	40–42	
Handling non-responsive groups	11	12–15	
Handling the cynic	4	5–6	
Handling 'side-trackers'	16	17–18	
Handling the 'know-it-all'	27	28–30	
Handling the 'lazy trainee/avoider'	34	35–38	
Handling the 'questioner'	48	49–50	

	E-MAIL NUMBER		
TOPIC	PROBLEM	SOLUTIONS	ALSO SEE...
Handling the 'joker'	57	58–59	
Handling the 'moaner'	67	68–69	
Handling the trainee who refuses to join in	76	77–79	
Handling the 'technophobe'	94	95–97	
Handling the 'back-turner'	101	102	
Handling the person who fails the course	91	92–93	96
Role-playing (reactions to)	98	99–100	
Giving feedback to delegates			35–38
Self-study packages	80	81–83	
Action planning	107	108–110	
Evaluation			
Post-course evaluation methods	19	20–23	108–110
Levels of evaluation	31	32, 33	

Dear Colleague: Setting the scene

From:	sara@e-mail.com
To:	jackie@e-mail.com
Date:	8 April
Subject:	Yesterday

Hello

Just a note to say how great it was to see you at the conference yesterday, and to have a chance to catch up on all the news. It seems so long ago since we worked together, and yet, in some ways, it's still very fresh in my memory. I know we had our moments, and we certainly weren't the easiest four people to manage; but, driving home last night, it occurred to me that we had a lot of good experiences as well.

As I said yesterday, I'm back training after two years in a generalist HR role, and I think I'm going to enjoy it. I'm the only trainer for the company, and report to the head of personnel. The team comprises of two personnel officers and an administrator. I know we talked about it yesterday, but I really miss having other trainers about – sometimes the others in the team look at me as if I'm crazy! They don't really know what I do. From what you said, it sounds like you appreciate what I mean. Are trainers really a breed of their own?

Your idea of us trying to support each other was really good. Please feel free to e-mail me anytime about what's happening at your end, any good ideas you come across or just to keep in touch.

Regards
Sara

E-mail

From: jackie@e-mail.com

To: sara@e-mail.com

Date: 8 April

Subject: Yesterday

Hello Sara

Thank you for your e-mail – it was good to see you too.

After some months of working alone in the training role I've been starved of, not intelligent conversation, but someone to put ideas to who does not wonder which spaceship I've beamed down from. So you're absolutely right when you say that I can appreciate what you're saying.

I think that the best way forward with our 'support network' would be not to set up anything rigid, but to get in touch as and when we feel we need to. I often have situations where I'm wondering 'What on earth do I do next?' and I'd really appreciate knowing that you're on the other end of the e-mail to ask. I think e-mail is going to be better than phone calls because we'll be able to reply when we're not rushed off our feet. If your working day is anything like mine, you'll know that when interrupted by the phone you can't always give the positive response that's needed.

So… keep in touch… I will and we'll soon have this training thing licked!

All the very best
Jackie

Dear Trainer: 110 problem-solving e-mails

From:	jackie@e-mail.com
To:	sara@e-mail.com
Sent:	19 April
Subject:	Distressed trainer from Essex

Dear Sara

I consider that I've been employed by my organization as a professional trainer and therefore I am qualified to offer specialist advice. I also know that I can't do everything and that a large part of my role is about encouraging departments and managers to take responsibility for the training of their staff.

I was very pleased when one department manager came to me and said that she was going to put together a training package for a group of her team leaders. I offered my support, which was gratefully acknowledged, but not accepted. This conversation took place several months ago and, to be honest, events overtook me and I didn't follow up on the situation. I've now received a copy of the training package and have a bit of a sticky situation to deal with. Whilst the ideas behind the programme are sound, I don't think the objectives are realistic or measurable. Names – including mine – have been allocated to sessions with no discussion about the sessions' content or the context of the learning that will take place. It's very obvious that the programme has been put together by a non-training person who is unfamiliar with all the ideas about teaching and learning. I have to say that this makes me feel a bit needed (!), but how on earth am I going to give feedback to the people involved without destroying a good working relationship and without coming across as a kill-joy or know-it-all?

Please help.

Regards
Jackie

From: sara@e-mail.com

To: jackie@e-mail.com

Sent: 20 April

Subject: Distressed trainer from Essex

Dear Jackie

Thanks for your e-mail, sorry to hear that work is causing some headaches! It's good news that this department manager has prepared a programme – how often are we told that the department managers will look after training themselves and then nothing happens?

However, standards must be upheld! My advice to you is to arrange a meeting with this manager, maybe over lunch, to give feedback and discuss the programme. The 'review' technique would form an excellent agenda for such a meeting. Work from the positive first, spending time saying what is good about the programme, what you do like and what aspects impress you (ie what works and why). Doing this first will help build trust and rapport with the manager, so that she won't think you're there only to criticize. This will make it easier to give the next message – what doesn't work and why.

As the training specialist, you're in a strong position, and should adopt a coaching role, rather than a critical 'I know best' position. Assume this manager has done her best and doesn't know any other way, so therefore should be given credit for what she has done. I always find this a useful approach.

When talking about the things you'd like to change, just pick a couple of areas that need working on – pick the most important. If you pick on any more than two or three areas, it may look as if you're trying to rewrite the programme completely, and this is likely to bring you into conflict with the manager. Working on the two or three most significant development areas gets improvement plus the opportunity for another feedback session at a later date. Also, you are still leaving the manager's pride intact!

It seems that you really have to give the feedback – that's the only way you can ensure that this and other programmes are consistent with your overall strategy and standards. ...

... As I write this, I'm imagining myself in your shoes – and I'd want to prepare by asking myself the following questions:

1. What is good about the programme and why?
(Points here could include simply the fact that the programme exists, or details like its content, layout or the methods used).

2. What changes are necessary to the programme?
    – Can I prioritize these into changes that are essential, useful and nice to have?
    – Which are the ones I feel very strongly about?
    – Why are these changes required?
    – What will these changes add to the programme?
    – Are they really required or do they just represent my way of doing things? (Why argue about the details of the programme if the end result will be the same as I want?)

3. How will the manager react when I explain why I want things changed? If the answer is negatively, how can I express the point differently to get a more positive response? The comment 'I don't like...', could become 'When I read this section, I felt...'; 'This is not right because there are no aims and objectives', could become 'It's a great programme... to make it consistent with the style of other programmes, we need to just add some aims and objectives'.

Hope this helps – let me know if you would like to discuss further or even practise before you meet.

Regards
Sara

From: jackie@e-mail.com

To: sara@e-mail.com

Sent: 10 January

Subject: Result??

Dear Sara

I had to write to update you on the situation that we discussed over the e-mail last year. I think that this one will make you smile (wryly).

I contacted you when I'd received a training programme prepared by one of our managers, but it wasn't really a full training programme and I was wondering how to address the situation with the manager without offending her.

I have to say that the advice you gave me was very sound. However, many other things came across my desk and 'talk to Sue about her training programme' got pushed further and further down my 'to do' list, until it fell off the bottom!

Like all things that you put off doing, this one has come back to bite me on the posterior. Last month I was approached by a different manager from the same department. He told me he'd been put in charge of the training programme for the team leaders and he'd like some help formulating it. I asked him whether he'd spoken with Sue and he said that she'd given him all her files. She told him she'd be happy to help with the programme, but if the powers that be don't want her to then she's happy to keep out of it.

It sounded to me as if Sue was feeling slightly aggrieved and I certainly felt guilty that I hadn't followed up on the issue sooner.

The other thing that John, the second manager, told me was that his department had recently lost a newly appointed team leader. During her exit interview the team leader said that she was leaving because she hadn't received the training she'd been promised at interview. And guess what that training was?

So the issue of this particular training programme had now become top priority since we obviously don't want to risk losing the other four team leaders, all appointed with the same promise of training. ...

... I decided to sit down with John and Sue to agree a plan. The first thing I asked was why the programme had never got off the ground (hoping they would not say 'Because you never came back to us about it'). What Sue actually said was 'I'd done the bit I was asked to do and I was waiting for Stuart (department manager) to tell me what to do next'. Oh well, at least I was off the hook, but it did make me wonder if I ought to be doing some management development involving forward planning and taking the initiative!

Anyway, that's all history now. So after some discussion, we came up with a plan as follows:

Sue and John will work together on specific aims and objectives for each session forming part of the programme. I gave them guidance on writing objectives ie to make sure that they are specific; measurable; realistic and achievable in terms of the resources available, the participants' availability and abilities; and timed.

Sue, John and I are going to meet with the four remaining team leaders to assure them that we're working on the formal training programme and to find out from them what immediate training and learning needs they have. Then we'll put together a personal development plan for each person.

Once Sue and John have set the objectives for each session within the programme, I'll help them to decide on the most appropriate methods to achieve those objectives.

Sue and John are going to work with each of their team leaders using a 'reflective journal'. Each person will be encouraged to make notes each week about situations they've dealt with that went well or went badly. They will then meet with Sue or John each month to discuss these situations and the learning that can come from the experiences.

So this is our initial plan. I just wish I hadn't left the situation to fester because getting Sue back on side took a huge effort and we lost a member of staff who was turning into a real asset to the department.

At least we have all learnt from the experience – although it's been costly. By the way, do you have any books about formulating budgets and budgetary control in your library? I've just been asked to put together the training budget for the next year and I've never done it before.

Jackie

From: sara@e-mail.com

To: jackie@e-mail.com

Sent: 28 April

Subject: The cynic

Dear Jackie

My first training class for some time – and I had a difficult person!

I was giving a half-day course on the company's appraisal system. I asked what experience everyone had of appraisal; they are all managers. The answers were very mixed. Bob said that he had been a manager for 12 years and had seen every appraisal going.

He gave good answers about how to use our appraisal form. The problem arose when we got to the final grading of performance. He became very cynical – almost argumentative. He said that everyone who worked for him was underpaid and, therefore, he had to give them good grades so that they would get good bonuses, regardless of how they actually performed. He wouldn't be told that this was wrong, and neither would he let us move on from the subject. I felt useless, as I didn't know how to get him to stop or convince him he was wrong.

Please help.

Sara

From: jackie@e-mail.com

To: sara@e-mail.com

Sent: 28 April

Subject: The cynic

Dear Sara

The problem you've described is both serious and sensitive. You mustn't feel that you're useless since you were dealing with cynicism and with the issue of a person admitting to committing a very serious act.

Taking the cynicism first, this is a problem that all trainers face at some time. One of the ways to deal with a person who constantly questions the validity of what you're saying is to ask the other members of the group for their opinions and experiences. There's a very good chance that in every group there'll be at least one positive person and you can use them to counter the arguments of your cynic.

An important tactic is for you to politely thank the person for his contribution and firmly say that you need to move on. Offer your time after the session so that the discussion can be continued in private. If you feel that you'll need to seek advice on an issue, make an appointment with the person for the next day.

Another thing you can try is to have a set of ground rules that are agreed at the start of the session. One of these rules could be something along the lines of 'if a discussion or issue can obviously not be dealt with in the session, then the topic should be noted and held for further discussion on a one-to-one basis'. Another way to describe this is to have a 'car park' where issues that are not part of the session can be left.

You mention in you e-mail that you 'didn't know... how to convince him he was wrong'. I would suggest that your role in the session was to make him think about his actions, not to convince him of anything. As a trainer you can't physically change ideas, only the individuals within your group can do that. Your role is to ask probing questions, to act as a catalyst for changing ideas and attitudes. You are not to blame if Bob or anyone else is not ready to change. ...

… The second issue you were dealing with was a person disclosing information to you that you would need to act upon. If Bob really was giving falsely high grades in order to get bonuses for his staff, he was abusing a system and in effect stealing from the company. This issue must be investigated further. You need to make it clear to the individual that you will be taking action. You also need to make it clear to the group that, with a pay-related appraisal system, objectivity is paramount.

The actions of this individual also bring into question the appraisal process itself. I would suggest that your organization needs to look at how grades are verified. One individual should not be able to authorize gradings without some reference to an objective person.

I hope this helps. Let me know what you decide to do.

Jackie

E-mail 6

From:	sara@e-mail.com
To:	jackie@e-mail.com
Sent:	4 May
Subject:	The cynic

Dear Jackie

Thanks for the advice about Bob, the cynical line manager from the appraisal course. As the course was only for a half-day, I haven't been able to address the issue as part of the programme, but I will remember your advice should I ever be faced with someone like this again, especially the bit about using ground rules and the rest of the group.

I was, however, still unhappy about his comments about giving maximum bonuses to his staff. To be honest, I was also a little worried when you pointed out that I should act on the information because he is actually stealing from the company – I hadn't even thought about that side of things!

Anyway, I decided to do two things:

I spoke to my manager, the head of personnel. As he's responsible for the bonuses, he said that he's going to make a note to check the bonuses Bob forwards for payment. If they seem unusually high, or out of step with what he knows about Bob's staff, he's going to question it with Bob's manager.

I arranged to see Bob. During the meeting, I said that I'd noticed he sounded very negative during the appraisal course and was there a problem? He actually apologized for 'giving me a hard time'. Apparently, he really believes his staff are underpaid and is concerned that his manager will not hear that message. We had a long conversation about why and how he believed this; resulting in me suggesting that he writes a full business proposal on what he thinks the salaries should be – I offered to help him draft it. I also advised him to copy it to my boss if he thought his own would block it. ...

... I don't know if he will do the report, but I do feel that I've built a better working relationship with him and a clearer understanding of him. I think the next time he's in my class I'll be more confident about addressing his negative behaviour at the time.

Thanks for the help.
Sara

From: sara@e-mail.com

To: jackie@e-mail.com

Sent: 17 May

Subject: AHHHH! – I'M SO ANNOYED!

I'm so annoyed I think I'm going to scream! John, our wonderful administrator is driving me crazy! I've just got a copy of the joining instructions he sent out for my course tomorrow, and he hasn't asked delegates to bring copies of their performance objectives with them. The whole of the first part of the workshop is based on reviewing them against the corporate priorities.

I also discovered that John hasn't ordered the video for the afternoon – he says he didn't know I needed it!

Perhaps I should cancel the whole thing, as it's obviously doomed. Next time, I'll organize it myself! What would you do?

Sara

From: jackie@e-mail.com

To: sara@e-mail.com

Sent: 17 May

Subject: AHHHH! – I'M SO ANNOYED!

Sara – don't panic...

Can the situation be resolved? I think cancelling should be your last resort since your delegates will have arranged their schedules to attend the course. Can you e-mail them and ask them to bring the information with them? Could your administrator get the information from somewhere else?

As for the video, you never know, the company may be able to courier it to you if you explain the situation – get your administrator to make the calls.

The main thing is to make sure that this never happens again. Your administrator obviously needs some feedback – don't talk with him now, as you'll probably end up losing your temper! (you know what you can be like!). I suggest you set a date to meet and then go through exactly what went wrong today and the consequences. I think with all the running around you'll make him do today, the consequences will be very obvious!

Go into coaching mode. Work with the administrator to produce a checklist for organizing training events. Here's the one that I use.

Send to the delegates:

• Joining instructions (include start and finish time, date, venue, food, accommodation).
• Pre-course work.
• Details of items to bring.

Ask the trainer:

• What will you need for each delegate?
• How many rooms will you require?
• Will you require a TV and video?
• Will you need a video camera?
• Will you need flipcharts? ...

Cont.

...
- Will you need an OHP?
- How do you want the room set up?

Book the venue:

- Book lunch and refreshments
- Book overnight accommodation
- Prepare handouts
- Prepare acetates
- Gather stationery
- Order videos
- Order activity materials

I have added to this checklist depending on the experience of the people I'm working with. You may want to amend it, but it gives you a basis to work from.

In the meantime, be calm – I'm sure your course will be fine.

Jackie

From: sara@e-mail.com

To: jackie@e-mail.com

Sent: 25 May

Subject: AHHHH! – I'M SO ANNOYED!

Thanks for the help last week – I did manage to save the course! John e-mailed and phoned the trainees and all but one turned up with the right information. And your idea about having the video sent to us by courier was inspired, and expensive!

The course actually was a great success, and the participants have gone off to put into practice their learning about performance objectives and perform-ance measurement. Having good evaluation forms calmed me down, so the day after the course I was able to sit and discuss the problems with John.

You would have been proud of me – instead of shouting and ranting about the problems, I did a model feedback session, following the three-stage method (you know: what the problem was, the effect it had, and the need to find a way to ensure that this never happens again).

It turns out that he has never been told exactly what delegates on this course needed – whilst he knew that it was his job to order equipment, I hadn't done a very good job of explaining what I needed and why.

As we talked it became more and more obvious that the problem was really that he didn't know enough about training to be more pro-active in his role, yet he seemed interested. I showed him your checklist and asked if he thought something like that would be useful. He's going to adapt it for us, and I will fill it in whenever I do a new course. In return, he asked if he could sit in on some of the courses, to see what I do and why. Of course, I said 'Yes'.

I'm training off-site next week and have suggested that he come to the first half-day, so that he gets a taste for what happens and how crucial the administration bit is. He is going to make me sit down every two weeks with him and ensure that he knows what to order.

Thanks for the advice.

Sara

From: sara@e-mail.com

To: jackie@e-mail.com

Sent: 6 June

Subject: AHHHH! – I'M SO ANNOYED!

Jackie

Remember the issues I had with my administrator, John? Thought you might like to see this e-mail he sent me today – looks like the effort paid off!

E-mail to sara@e-mail.com

Sara

I just wanted to thank you for letting me attend your course last week – it really helped me to understand how our two jobs link together. I've only been doing this job for a few months and no one had fully explained this to me. I've drawn up the checklists for each course and have ordered the things you said you needed. Perhaps when you are free, you could review them with me.

Regards
John

From:	jackie@e-mail.com
To:	sara@e-mail.com
Sent:	20 May
Subject:	You think you have problems!

Dear Sara

I've been working with a group today and I don't know what's going on. The workshop was about communication skills – and as far as I'm concerned the participants have none! This might be a bit unfair (as you may be able to tell, I'm a bit irritated with them), because when I gave them a couple of written exercises they lapped them up. But unfortunately most of my material is based on discussion; small group work with feedback and role-play.

Most of the time when I asked a question to try and prompt some discussion, the group just sat there and looked at me. I began to wonder if I had something in my hair or if I was speaking another language. I know for sure that the people in this group are very intelligent individuals, so I'm at a loss to know what's going on. I've got to run part two of the workshop next week and I'm really dreading it – have you got any thoughts or suggestions that you think might help me?

How did you get on with your course the other day – did it go ahead?

Write soon, I need some help here.

Jackie

From:	sara@e-mail.com
To:	jackie@e-mail.com
Sent:	21 May
Subject:	You think you have problems!

Dear Jackie

Isn't it worrying when the group doesn't communicate or give you anything back! These are the sort of groups I hate the most – I feel like asking is anyone in the group learning? Am I talking to myself? Is this a load of rubbish?

I remember some time ago, actually when we used to work together, I was training on a residential weekend. By Saturday afternoon, I was really concerned because the group were behaving exactly as you describe. It was Dave that helped me..

At the tea break, I was desperate. He listened and then offered some good advice. He said there were three potential reasons for such behaviour:

• Participants did not want to be on the course, and were doing the minimum to get by.
• The course wasn't meeting their needs.
• Their learning style was reflective/theorist – and everything was OK.

I had started the session by spending quite a long time on their personal objectives and what they were hoping to get out of it. You remember what it was like in those days – we didn't have any true background information on the people attending the courses, they just arrived. These days, as an in-house trainer, at least I know the delegates and what they do, which makes life a bit easier as I have some clue to personalities, experience, etc. Anyway, I was happy that the material I was covering was what they wanted, so that didn't seem to be the problem.

So, two other possibilities. I decided to establish their learning styles first. With reflectors/theorists, they often have learnt the information but don't need to discuss it. Reflectors don't always perform well in discussions, as they need to sit and think about their answers. Once theorists understand the concepts and models, they are ready to move on to the next intellectual ...

... challenge, and therefore might not willingly discuss areas they think they understand. So in my case, I set a quiz. Result! They all got top marks. So the training was obviously working! With my new vision, I started to watch them more carefully, and overall, I did seem to have a high percentage of reflectors. With this in mind, I moved some of the exercises to apply the techniques to the next day and included some of the information at the end of the evening about what we were going to do tomorrow – giving them the chance to reflect overnight. As Dave said: if they're learning what they need to, don't push them into displaying it in an unnatural style. Just work with and accept their preference.

You might want to give everyone in your group a learning styles questionnaire, especially if you're doing communication skills. You can link this to how different people learn and communicate, and why if two people have different styles, communication is sometimes not effective, etc etc. Also send out some pre-course work before your next session.

That night over dinner I was able to explore why people were on the course – a casual question like 'How did you hear about the course?' gave me lots of information about whether they had selected it or had been sent on it. (If it's not a residential course you can always have a coffee break with them.)

And yes, my course did go ahead and it was successful, despite all the admin issues!

Let me know how your communication session goes.

Regards – and thanks for the advice.

Sara

From: jackie@e-mail.com

To: sara@e-mail.com

Sent: 26 May

Subject: Hi!

Thanks for your suggestion about my non-communicative group. I decided to try the learning styles questionnaire on them and I did find out, as you had suggested, that they are all very high on the reflective scores.

I did try to take this on board so that I wasn't so personally affected when they did not talk to me. I have to say though, because of my style of training, I found it very difficult to use techniques that did not involve group discussion – and when I did, the group found it difficult to participate. One thing I did find was that they were more willing to talk in smaller groups and in pairs, so I'll remember that.

I made sure I gave lots of handouts and opportunities for the participants to write their own notes and to consider how what we had been talking about could be applied in their work.

However, I am still a little disappointed about the way the course went. I still feel that I didn't achieve the aim of improving their communication skills.

Jackie

From: sara@e-mail.com

To: jackie@e-mail.com

Sent: 26 May

Subject: Reflectors

I don't like training them either! Perhaps we should do a study of known reflectors – how do you like to learn? Then again...perhaps not!

Yours as a pragmatist
Sara

From: jackie@e-mail.com

To: sara@e-mail.com

Sent: 7 September

Subject: Reflectors

Do you remember the group I was working with who were doing a course on communication skills and who would not communicate with me? And do you remember how disappointed I was when they still did not want to participate in group discussions, even at the end of the course?

Well, I've had a really interesting experience with one of the participants from the group and it has restored my confidence and my faith in learning theory!

One of the participants in the group has recently been promoted from supervisor to first-line manager. Last week she came to me to talk about her personal development plan and she brought up the topic of the communication skills course. When she told me how much she had enjoyed the course, I nearly fell off my chair! She was the quietest member of the group and never really looked happy to be there.

She went on to say that she often refers back to the handouts I gave out and that she has started to keep a journal of her experiences in her new role in order to help her reflect and develop.

She has even asked me to run the communication skills course again for her five administrative staff who will soon be having a great deal more interface with internal customers.

A success I feel! Just wanted to let you know – I feel really chuffed!

Jackie

From: jackie@e-mail.com

To: sara@e-mail.com

Sent: 6 June

Subject: How do you stop wandering trainees?

I'm really hoping you'll be able to help me with what is becoming a real problem.

I'm working with a group on a monthly basis giving a supervisor's development course. At the start of the first session I felt that it was important to give the participants an opportunity for discussion – to consider some of the things that would help them put into practice the skills they were learning, and also some of the things that would get in the way. This was fine and a whole range of issues emerged.

I've just run the fourth session with the group and I am really concerned about several comments that I've received on the reaction sheets. People are saying things like 'We need to stick to the topic at hand', 'The group keeps going on to the same old issues', and 'We could be out by lunchtime if we did not discuss so many unrelated items'.

Now I know I do let the group go on to topics that are not really related to the session title but it's not as if we're discussing the weather – quite often we are talking about the issues that will affect supervisors every day, such as company culture, the management style of the company and communication issues. I believe that the participants do not often have the chance to raise their concerns and that I should provide them with this opportunity.

Having said this, it now does seem to be a problem for a number of people in the group. My question is how can I bring people back to the topic at hand without making them feel that I am trivializing what they have to say? What do you think? Have you ever been in this situation? Am I being very passive? How can I take control of the situation? Please let me have your thoughts.

Jackie

From: sara@e-mail.com

To: jackie@e-mail.com

Sent: 8 June

Subject: How do you stop wandering trainees?

When I read your e-mail, I started to think: 'Oh s***, I don't know'. Then I started to think about techniques for managing discussions.

If a group is going off-track, say 'This is not strictly the subject we were going to talk about, but I can see it's a big issue – would you like to spend time talking about it now or shall we do that over coffee?'.

Or you could say 'We don't have time for that now, it's not relevant to everyone so I'm going to park it and we will discuss it over lunch'.

Another favourite of mine is 'I'm happy to explore this with you, but I think we need to do it outside this group…'.

But although these are good techniques, they're not going to help you with the fact that some of your group dislike the fact that discussions have wandered off-track before. How would you feel about starting the next session with a review of the feedback? You could put up or give out a summary of the feedback reaction sheets and say that you want to discuss it and agree any resulting action. If you do this, you have to be in listening mode, saying something like: 'One of the areas I would like to clarify is this one about not keeping to the subject – can you (group) tell me more about this?'.

Encourage the group to tell you and then, after they have shared and discussed, ask how they would like all of you to deal with this in future. They might agree to allow it or take responsibility for stopping it.

I think this is a particularly good technique for supervisors and line managers – we should be showing them how to evaluate feedback properly and act on it, not just hear feedback and not refer to it again.

Let me know what you do.

Sara

From: jackie@e-mail.com

To: sara@e-mail.com

Sent: 12 September

Subject: How do you stop wandering trainees?

I've had a bit of a revelation about why I allow groups to divert from the original subject!

I've realized that the reason groups of managers and supervisors want to talk about all their issues when they come to a training course is that they don't get the opportunity to do this at any other time. We're constantly saying we should improve communication and it seems to me that maybe we should be setting up some informal groups to do this.

What I've suggested to the senior managers is that they encourage their managers and supervisors to create informal networks. For example, some managers have decided that every month they'll get together over breakfast in the canteen to simply exchange news and views. Another group has arranged to go out to the pub after work every week. These informal meetings have really improved communication in the groups concerned and since they began, three months ago, the groups have grown and have become more and more cross-functional.

I've also been really lucky in that I'm now able to book a table in the canteen for my participants and have encouraged them to all go to lunch together. The training department doesn't pay for lunch, but most of the participants have felt that it is worth staying together to 'chew the fat' over lunch (no pun intended – the food in our canteen is actually quite good!).

The other thing I've started to do when I'm running sessions on new policy and procedures (which is quite often at the moment) is to arrange to meet with the managers prior to seeing their supervisors and staff. This way I can introduce the new material and the managers can sort out any logistical issues they might have in implementing the policy and procedure. I then send the managers away with the brief that they must discuss these issues with any participants who are coming on to the courses. In an extreme case, this has enabled me to cut a full-day course down to a half-day, purely because the participants were fully briefed and sure that their managers would support them in the implementation. ...

Cont.

... I really feel this is a step forward in having line managers involved in the training and coaching process. We've been able to smoothly implement changes and managers feel they're more involved in what used to be HR-driven issues. I suppose this is what the textbooks mean when they talk about devolving HR to the line!

Sara, please don't think that all is perfect in my company and in my training room – I know we still have a long way to go, but I'm finding that I'm more able to say 'this is not an issue for this particular session' because I know that participants will have the opportunity to discuss issues elsewhere.

Hope all is well with you.

Jackie

From: sara@e-mail.com

To: jackie@e-mail.com

Sent: 9 June

Subject: Evaluation

Thanks for the phone call – I feel much better now.

I'm interested in knowing how you evaluate your courses and workshops. At the end of each course I've been using a reaction questionnaire which has a mixture of tick boxes and spaces for other comments. The questionnaire asks what people thought of the presentation, and allows comments on the venue and administration, as well as whether their personal objectives were met.

It seems to me that most of the comments that I get are very positive – even when I know in my heart of hearts that the session has not gone well. I think this is also partly why I was very sensitive about the negative feedback – when line mangers were telling me that the training didn't cover all the areas, yet comments on the evaluation forms were good. I want to try and get better feedback from the trainees, rather than wait until the next management meeting. Any thoughts?

Sara

From: jackie@e-mail.com

To: sara@e-mail.com

Sent: 19 June

Subject: Evaluation

Sara

I know exactly what you mean – I got to the stage where I realized that most people really just want to be nice at the end of a course, or else they do not comment at all. The other thing is that people are so tired after a day of training that they simply want to go home.

I've now started to ask participants to work in small groups or pairs to answer the same 'reaction-type' questions that I used to put on the reaction questionnaire. I've found that I now get slightly more constructive feedback. The other thing I'm doing is asking each delegate's line manager to set up a meeting during which the individual's objectives are reviewed and it's discussed how the course learning will be applied. Sometimes I don't get a written response from these meetings; however, following them up with a phone call to the manager and the delegate has started to give me some very useful feedback. It also prompts those who haven't held their meeting to do so.

The main thing that has helped me improve the quality of my evaluation is that I've started to go and see the participants in their working environment and talk to them about how they're applying their learning. This is time-consuming, but it does help and I'm often able to do some coaching whilst I'm there. I'm also developing much better relationships with the line managers and through this I'm able to encourage them to help their people learn. After all, it's often the line manager who requests the training and therefore I believe he or she should participate in the process of ensuring that the training is effective.

An idea I intend to try in the near future sounds a bit trendy, but I think it might work for long-term programmes. I'm going to try working with some 'focus groups' – small groups of participants from the programmes who have been selected either because I know they will be constructive or because they have very strong negative or positive views about the training. I'll get these people together for a couple of hours and review the ...

... programme with them, asking them about objectives, content, methods and so on. I'll let you know how this goes – or if you try it, you can let me know!

I also use action plans. I ask each participant to complete an action plan at the end of the course, take a copy and then send the copy back to the participant and his or her manager 6–8 weeks after the course. This reminds the person of what they were going to do with their learning and may encourage the line manager to follow up with the participant.

Keep me informed of any other ideas that you hear about since I also find evaluation a bit of a minefield!

Regards
Jackie

From:	jackie@e-mail.com
To:	sara@e-mail.com
Sent:	27 June
Subject:	Evaluation

Dear Sara

I've just remembered some other ways I evaluate training. At the start of a session I ask delegates to write down their objectives for the training. Then at the end of the session we discuss if the objectives have been achieved. A variation of this would be to get participants to discuss objectives in small groups and then give feedback – but this does take longer.

I've also sent out a pre-course questionnaire to participants with the stated objectives for the course. This asks people what they hope to gain from the programme and how this will benefit them in their current role and in the future. Once again, these are discussed at the start and the end of the programme.

If I think of any more ideas, I'll send them to you.

Jackie

From: sara@e-mail.com

To: jackie@e-mail.com

Sent: 30 July

Subject: Evaluation

Dear Jackie

I've been working on the evaluation ideas and think it's working! I regularly use end-of-course group exercises; my favourite two are:

- Completing unfinished sentences. I give trainees part of a sentence to complete such as 'Today, I have enjoyed…' or 'I am planning to use…'. The group then share each trainee's comments.
- Written comments from trainees in small groups. I ask them to write on a flipchart what they've learnt and how they'll use it.

I've also been working with my administrator (we're getting on quite well these days) to agree a procedure for sending out evaluation forms – within a week of the course, he sends the form to the participants. They have to complete it and discuss it with their line managers. John then summarizes the returned forms for me – I review the summary and if necessary the actual forms. I've also just tried your idea of focus groups. We've done an extensive programme involving training about 60 people across the company. I got the administrator to select four groups of six people from the participants and invited them to take part in a focus group. During the focus group meetings we talked about the programme, its content and how it's changed the participants' performance. This really worked well and I was a little surprised by how willing participants were to talk to me. The feedback showed that not everyone has been successful applying their learning, so I'm going to run some follow-up workshops for anyone who'd like to attend.

The other big area of learning for us is that in two departments, the line managers are not spending time with trainees before the courses agreeing learning objectives. I've decided that there is only so much nagging a trainer can do! I've got three people from these departments on courses next month, so I've asked for meetings with their line managers prior to the courses to agree training objectives. …

... These groups worked so well that I think I'll do them again. They are quite time-consuming, so I will probably reserve them for the larger programmes.

Thanks for the idea.

By the way, are you going to the conference?

Sara

From:	jackie@e-mail.com
To:	sara@e-mail.com
Sent:	3 August
Subject:	Evaluation

Dear Sara

Thank you for your e-mail. I also tried focus groups but it was a bit of a let-down!

I managed to get together a selection of participants who'd completed a supervisors' development programme with me. There were 12 participants in total, from different groups and different departments.

The first problem I encountered was that even though they had all completed the same programme, they didn't know each other and weren't particularly willing to share thoughts and ideas in an open forum.

Well, having done a couple of icebreakers with them, I split them into small groups (four people in each) and gave them a list of questions to consider:

- What knowledge did you gain from the development programme?
- What skills did you gain from the programme?
- How are you applying the knowledge and skills gained in your daily work?
- What is supporting you in applying the knowledge and skills?
- What is hindering you from applying the knowledge and skills?
- What do you feel would be an appropriate follow-up to the programme?

I gave them an hour to complete the task and then took feedback in the plenary group. While they were working I did circulate and try to keep them on track, but I found that the discussions kept wandering to company performance, general gossip and a wide range of moans. Then to cap it all I ran out of time in the plenary group. Also, I hadn't made it clear what notes I wanted from the small group work, so I was left with little usable written information.

What did I learn from this? ...

Cont.

...
1. If possible, have participants from the same training group in each focus group.
2. Keep the focus group small enough to lead the discussion myself.
3. Ensure that complete notes are made from discussions.

I will try this again – I think!

See you soon.

Jackie

From: jackie@e-mail.com

To: sara@e-mail.com

Sent: 21 August

Subject: How to handle disagreements

Sara

I have a slight problem – I think I may be playing 'piggy in the middle' with an employee and her manager.

One of our long-standing managers has told me she's having problems understanding our budgeting process and thinks she should go on a basic accounting course. I started to dig out some information about courses and then I thought – 'Hang on a minute, I really should discuss this with her manager'. I'm glad I did!

Having spoken to her manager, I'm not sure this is simply about accounting and budgeting. It seems to me there are other issues this manager needs to address first such as dealing with her team members, communication and running meetings. Apparently these are real problems which were pointed out at her appraisal. However, she doesn't seem to have taken this on board and is focusing on a completely different issue.

How should I manage the disagreement between these two whilst still maintaining the good relationship that I have developed with both parties?

Jackie

From:	sara@e-mail.com
To:	jackie@e-mail.com
Sent:	22 August
Subject:	How to handle disagreements

Dear Jackie

I don't envy you this one. Part of me thinks you need to be seen to meet her request so that she continues to trust you; however, courses are expensive and if her manager is not going to support it, then it could end up being a waste of time. Is there someone in the company, such as an accountant, who could talk her through the company process? I always think this is a good solution as it can really focus on company procedures and processes, when an external course will be generic. Then I suppose there are three options:

- Meet with her and her manager to discuss and agree a specific training plan to cover all her needs.
- Go through her appraisal with her, and ask how she is meeting the needs contained in it – she might not want to agree to weaknesses in a meeting including her manager.

What is the process for actioning needs from the appraisal? In my company, it's normal practice for us to read appraisals and allocate training automatically – although it does cause a few problems when people get their joining instructions!

- Tell her manager that he or she and this person need to sort it out between them. The question here is – how competent is the manager?!

Personally, I like the upfront, open approach of the first option, but you'll need to handle it carefully.

Sara

From: jackie@e-mail.com

To: sara@e-mail.com

Sent: 27 August

Subject: How to handle disagreements

Dear Sara

Thanks for your advice on how to deal with a disagreement between an employee and her line manager. Having considered all the options, I decided that the best thing to do would be tackle the situation head on. I chose the first option from your list. I was absolutely terrified prior to the meeting – as you know, I'm one of those people who likes to stay on the right side of everyone and I could see that I had the potential to really upset the employee or the manager. However, I took a few deep breaths and went for it...

I felt a bit like a marriage guidance counsellor when we were all sitting together in the room. I managed to find a room without a desk, but with some comfortable chairs arranged around a low coffee table. This may sound a bit strange, but I am sure that this environment made a difference. It certainly helped me to relax and the meeting seemed much less formal than it would have done in an office at a desk.

I opened the meeting by explaining why we were there and what I wanted to achieve from the meeting – ie to clarify what the real training needs of the individual (Ann) were and to produce a plan to address them. I asked Ann and Chris (her manager) for their views on what they wanted to achieve from the meeting and they both agreed with me! A great start.

I'd asked Ann to bring a copy of her appraisal with her to the meeting so that we could review the needs that were raised there. We used the appraisal as the starting point for the discussion. I encouraged Ann to talk about the needs relating to her team, asking Chris to hold any comment until Ann had had the time to put all her comments forward. After some initial probing questions from me (eg how do you feel about the needs identified here? What have you been doing in order to address these needs? Which of the strategies you've used have worked and why? What have you tried that hasn't worked so well and why do you think this is?). Ann opened up and began to tell us her side of the story. I won't go into ...

... details here, but basically Ann had no real idea about how to address the people issues and so she had decided to focus on something she could really get a handle on – the budgeting process. She felt that this was something concrete that she needed to know more about.

Chris was really good at staying quiet while Ann spoke and when she had finished, thanked her for what she had said and apologized for not giving her more support with the team issues.

The outcome of the whole meeting was a plan which included Chris doing some coaching with Ann on the budgeting process and me setting up time to spend with her, in her working environment, to help her with the people issues. Once I've seen the way she works I'll do some one-to-one sessions with her to give feedback and encourage her to try some new ways of handling different situations.

Thanks to you I felt able to tackle this situation and it has all turned out beautifully.

Cheers
Jackie

From:	jackie@e-mail.com
To:	sara@e-mail.com
Sent:	2 September
Subject:	Participants

Dear Sara

Have you ever wanted to tell one of your participants to shut up and listen to someone else for a change?

I had this situation today (and I know it's going to happen the next time I meet this particular group). I did resist the urge to scream 'Just be quiet!' at the top of my voice, you'll be pleased to hear!

I was running a session with a group of 10 experienced managers. I had various activities planned and at the start of the session I wanted to do some input on various theories about the topic.

Well, as soon as I started, one of the delegates challenged what I was saying. 'Good', I thought, 'this'll be a good day with lots of healthy discussion'. Little did I know! About five minutes later another challenge – 'But what about the work of so and so,' the delegate said. Then came the first activity – 'Oh, I've done this one before, would you like me to help you with observation?' I declined the offer, and asked the participant to be part of the group, but not to give too much help. During the feedback session, comments came out such as 'When I did this the last time...', 'In my last company...'.

I could tell that the other participants were becoming restless and referred to our ground rule about allowing each person to have their say. I thanked the delegate for his comments and said maybe now would be a good time for others to comment.

I can't tell you how many times I referred to that ground rule!

What shall I do? This person has been there, done that and got the T-shirt, but I know from conversations with the line manager that this individual needs to learn and be performing much better within the very near future.

Any tips?

Jackie

From:	sara@e-mail.com
To:	jackie@e-mail.com
Sent:	4 September
Subject:	Participants

Dear Jackie

Yes I have! There are a number of reasons why this person may be behaving this way – all you have to do is establish which one it is and then act accordingly.

Firstly: you say 'this person has been there, done that and got the T-shirt, but I know from conversations with the line manager that this individual needs to learn and be performing much better' – which makes me wonder what the training need really is. Perhaps it's a case of someone knowing their stuff but not being able to implement it back in the workplace. Is this participant a theorist who's struggling applying learning? If this is the case, what feedback has there been from the manager? Does the person know there is a performance problem, or has he just been told to go on the training because everyone is going on it? It's unfortunate, but as you know, many managers fail to give good feedback. In an ideal trainer-led world, all line managers would be able to say to their staff, 'This is what you are not doing, I'm sending you on this course so you can learn, this is what I want you to be able to do at the end'. Most managers prefer the 'there's a course, go on it and see what you get out of it'. Now this is difficult to identify, because if you ask the manager he or she will swear that it's been done properly! I wonder whether this participant had clear objectives at the start of the course: was he clear about what he wanted to learn and do as a result of the training?

Let's assume that his personal objectives weren't clear. If I was in your shoes, I would have a little chat with the participant; something on the lines of: 'You obviously have a lot of experience, and I want to ensure that the training is meeting your needs and is at the right level for you. Talk to me about what you want to get from the course'. This may involve a coaching role asking questions like: What are the areas of this work/skill that you enjoy? What aspects do you dislike or find more difficult? If you have all these skills, why do you think your manager put you on the course? ...

... Another possibility is that the participant knows why he is on the course, but needs to get the attention from you and/or the others. This could just be because he likes the attention, or because he feels threatened and wants to show he's got something to offer. You could get him to 'help' you – say that you've noticed he has a lot of knowledge/experience and that you would value his help in training the others. Tell him that you need him to let others answer first (or whatever it is that you want him to do).

Another option is to address his behaviour and the problem it's causing you – have I told you about the three-step approach to feedback?

1. What is the person doing?
2. What is the result of that behaviour?
3. What do you want the person to do in the future?

For example: 'I noticed that you have said on several occasions that you have done these exercises before, so I'm concerned that you aren't learning anything new. Can we discuss this and, if it is the case, agree how we can move forward to make this work for you.'

Or: 'You obviously have a lot of experience – you refer to what you've done before and often give the answers before anyone else. This is great, however, I think some of the group are feeling restless because they're unable to contribute – I don't want you to stop contributing but we need to agree a way for everyone to get a fair chance.'

Personally, I would try a bit of all three – start with a chat about how experienced he is and what his objectives are and see where that takes you.

Let me know how it goes. Good luck.

Sara

From:	jackie@e-mail.com
To:	sara@e-mail.com
Sent:	20 September
Subject:	Participants

Dear Sara

Just wanted to let you know about how I got on with the person who would not listen to anyone else.

Basically I did what you suggested. I took him aside and explained to him that I was a bit concerned that the course may not be meeting his needs since he already seemed to have an awful lot of experience in the area being covered. I also asked him what his reasons were for booking the course in the first place.

What a response – I was glad that I was talking to him in private! He launched into a long monologue about the number of years he's been with the company, the number of changes he's seen and his dissatisfaction with 'these youngsters who want to tell him how to do his job'. Once he had got this all off his chest he apologized and explained that his manager, a man 20 years his junior, had sent him on the course 'because he hadn't done any training for the last 18 months'. He had tried to explain to the manager that he has done several similar courses in the past and had asked why the manager felt this training would benefit him. The manager had told him 'If I say you are going on a course, you go, not question'. At this point I began to see why he was being 'difficult'! Following this part of the discussion, I asked him how he would feel if I were to have a chat with his manager – he said OK and wished me luck. In the meantime, we agreed that he would remain with the group, he would share his experience, but not in such a forthright and overbearing way.

Are you wondering how I got on with the manager? I can tell you I wasn't looking forward to the meeting one little bit, but I took a deep breath, prepared my opening gambit and went for it.

What I found out was really interesting. The manager seems to be really supportive of this individual and wanted to show him how much he values his contribution to the team by offering him some development. ...

Cont.

... Unfortunately, when they were discussing this he simply said 'Alan, I want to send you on this course', at which point Alan seemed to over-react and the manager responded by over-reacting himself. He knew he'd made an error, but didn't know how to approach Alan without losing face – he obviously feels intimidated by the older man.

Well, I went into coaching mode and we talked about how he could approach Alan, explain the misunderstanding, then use questioning and listening techniques first to find out Alan's experience and then identify areas for development.

The manager has now tried this and, after a bit of a rocky start, he and Alan have been able to develop a good working relationship. Alan is no longer attending my course, but he has been booked on to an advanced technician's course in his specialist area.

For me, this just goes to prove that needs analysis at the front line is all-important. I wonder what you might be able to help me with on this issue...?

Jackie

From:	sara@e-mail.com
To:	jackie@e-mail.com
Sent:	11 November
Subject:	The know-it-all

Dear Jackie

Was it you who I was talking to about a participant who seemed to know it all? I've just had a similar situation and thought I would share the experience, as we say in the training world!

I was training a group of team leaders yesterday in module one of a four-module programme. Sean, one of the accountants, constantly talked throughout the day. It didn't matter what the subject was, or who else was talking; he had an opinion. A few times, I had to tell him that he'd made an inappropriate comment (usually about women!). This didn't matter, he still had an opinion. Sean is quite young and is very keen to get on. When he introduced himself at the start of the course and talked about why he was here, he said he was very eager to learn everything about management. He said (and I quote) 'I've got the right personality, which makes me a good manager, I want to know some of the theories'.

Initially I lived with it, but it became quite off-putting, especially when one of the others joined in – it became like 'The Little and Large Show'! I heard the others teasing him during the coffee break about how he always was talking. I sat next to him at lunch and it was quite clear to me that he just wanted to make a good impression.

After lunch, we did a group exercise, which resulted in them, as a group, storming. In the feedback session afterwards, he started not just to monopolize the discussion but to play the experience down. He was saying things like 'It wasn't that bad', and 'People are taking this too seriously'. He also attributed several of these thoughts to others. At that point, I stopped everyone and said that there appeared to be a lot of very useful feedback and learning, and that it would be a shame not to hear it properly. I said that we would go round the circle and give everyone a chance to say what had happened for them during the exercise: no one was to speak until it was their turn. ...

... I deliberately started at the end furthest away from Sean, so that he had to be quietest the longest. Midway through the first person's comments, he piped up to disagree. I told him that I'd purposely started at the other end of the group because he was very vocal, and I wanted to ensure that everyone had an opportunity to speak. I told him to listen and think about what people were saying and that if he wanted to respond, he could when it was his turn. I only had to tell him four times not to speak yet! Well, probably only three – the fourth time, I just lifted my hand as he started and he shut up!

During the feedback time, quite a lot came up about the effects different people had had on others and how different things were read into people's behaviours. There was also quite a lot of blame. When it came to Sean's turn, he said that everything he wanted to say had been said, but that having listened to everyone else he now saw that they hadn't worked together as a group and had ignored each others' feelings. He suggested they should agree that, faced with similar situations in future, they would not be so quick to try and start the activity, but make sure they invest time in planning how they would work together during the task.

I could have kissed him – a good leadership proposal without too much time and energy being spent on trivial and irrelevant comments! The group were all impressed too and someone said, 'That's the first interesting thing you've said all day'.

Afterwards, when we were doing the action plans, I told him that sometimes it was as if he needed to speak just to hear his own voice. I said that when he was made to stop talking and listen to others he was able to contribute much better to the group. He said he'd realized that if he stopped talking so much, he could think about what he wanted to say and make it more relevant. Needless to say, we agreed to put it on his action plan.

I'm not sure I should have used such a strict approach with a trainee, but in this case, it worked.

Regards
Sara

From: jackie@e-mail.com

To: sara@e-mail.com

Sent: 4 December

Subject: How to validate learning

Sara

I keep hearing the expressions 'validating' and 'evaluating' learning, and to be honest I am not sure I know the difference between them.

What do you think that these two terms mean? How do I go about doing them? My manager has asked me to put a proposal together about how we will validate and evaluate our current employee training programmes.

Jackie

From: sara@e-mail.com

To: jackie@e-mail.com

Sent: 8 December

Subject: Evaluating v validating

Jackie

The way I use these two terms is as follows:

VALIDATING is checking that the person has achieved the required standard, ie has learnt what they needed to know or do. For example, if someone is being taught shorthand, can they do the x words per minute? Validating exercises therefore, are quizzes, tests, simulated real work, subject-specific questions, assessment activities, etc.

EVALUATING is reviewing how effective the training event was. This includes looking at whether the objectives have been met and receiving feedback on the venue, administration, presentation, etc. This is also concerned with the training's effect on behaviour and performance.

I think validation takes place during the training and evaluating usually happens afterwards, and looks at how well the person has transferred the learning.

Does this make sense?

Sara

From: jackie@e-mail.com

To: sara@e-mail.com

Sent: 3 January

Subject: Evaluating v validating

Dear Sara

Thanks for explaining the difference between validation and evaluation so clearly and concisely. I've been doing some reading about evaluation and all that goes with it and I wonder if you could give me your feedback on my current thoughts…

As I understand it, validating is very much focused on the individual. Has he or she learnt what is needed during the training event? We validate learning by 'tests' at the end of the event. This to me is about checking whether the new knowledge and skills have been implanted into the short-term memory – conscious competence I suppose.

Evaluation is about whether the knowledge and skills have been applied in the 'real world' – ie have they moved from the short-term memory to the long-term memory? This is where the saying 'You can't train experience' seems to come from. This then must be about moving from the conscious competence to unconscious competence.

I also read something about different levels of evaluation. I believe that the original work on this was done by D L Kirkpatrick in the late 1950s. Recent updates to his model identify the following levels where evaluation takes place:

• Reactions
  Level 1 is carried out at the end of the training event to assess participants' initial reactions (often using 'happy sheets'). Reactions to various areas can be assessed, eg course presentation, venue, and achievement of objectives.

• Learning
  This is where participants consider what they actually learnt from the training event. …

...

- Changes in job performance
  At this level, focus is still on the individual and evaluation is about whether the person has been able to apply their learning to change the ways in which they work.

- Changes in departmental performance
  This is where the 'bigger picture' comes in. I see this level as being about how the change in the individual's performance affects the performance of his or her department.

- Changes in organizational performance
  At its final level, evaluation is about how the changes in individual and departmental performance affect the performance of the organization as a whole.

This all seems very well when I write it here, but I'm not really sure how to go about relating training events to departmental and organizational performance. It seems to me there will be many other factors that affect these areas. How then can we attribute improvements simply to a training event?

What do you think?

Jackie

From:	sara@e-mail.com
To:	jackie@e-mail.com
Sent:	10 February
Subject:	A lazy trainee

Dear Jackie

I've been training team leaders this week, and am a little concerned about the behaviour of one of my participants.

The course is very participative, with lots of group-work exercises and tasks to complete. I noticed half way through the first day that one guy, Tom, seemed to go to the toilet a lot! Well, I didn't think too much of it, as everyone has different needs!

Well, today is Day 4 and I've noticed that every time we start an exercise or split into groups he makes an excuse to leave the room and doesn't come back until the group has started or assigned roles. Sometimes he says it's to go to the toilet, sometimes for a smoke break, sometimes he doesn't say anything! It's almost like he's trying to avoid doing any work.

Any hints for how I deal with this lazy person?

Sara

From:	jackie@e-mail.com
To:	sara@e-mail.com
Sent:	12 January
Subject:	A lazy trainee

Dear Sara

Thank you for the e-mail. I sympathize with you. I had a person very much like the one you describe only last month. Here's what I tried:

After the person had avoided four or five activities, I decided that enough was enough and I called a break as soon as I could naturally fit one in. I asked the person to hang on for a moment as I had a message for him. Once I had the person on his own, I confronted the situation outright by saying 'I can't help but notice that you seem to be missing at the start of every group activity, is there a problem?'. At first he denied it, but when I said a second time 'I really do think that your absences at the start of each activity are more than coincidence', he admitted that he feels very uncomfortable working in small groups. Apparently he is dyslexic and has a real fear that he will be asked to write things down for the group. He goes off at the start of each activity so that he can avoid being nominated or simply passed the pen. I have to admit that I was really thrown by this at first, but I managed to pull myself together and we discussed the best way forward. I was able to get him to see that he has a great deal to offer in small group sessions since he is very experienced in our business. I also helped him to see that he may be missing out on some real learning opportunities. I suggested that rather than avoid the start of small group sessions, he be the one who takes charge and volunteers to do the feedback in the plenary session. He was actually quite happy to do this. I also said that I would find other methods of feedback, rather than using flipchart presentations each time.

Of course, your person may not have a problem such as I have described, but I certainly think that confronting him will be a good way to start to resolve the problem.

One of my colleagues has a person in a supervisory development group who has said that his knowledge is his alone – he has worked for it and he is …

... not about to share it with anyone else! This means that he also absents himself as much as possible from group work. My colleague has handled this by referring to one of our ground rules, which states 'give freely of your experience, others will have a great deal to learn from you'. Obviously we cannot make anyone do anything, however the whole group did agree to these ground rules at the start of the programme and should be prepared to be reminded of them.

I suppose that your final option would be to point out to the person that he's placing an unnecessary burden on his co-workers and if he doesn't wish to participate fully in the programme, regardless of the support that you are offering, you'll have no alternative but to ask him to return to work. You'll also have to make a report to his line manager. This might make a truly lazy person sit up and take notice!

Hope that one of these ideas will be of use to you – good luck!

Jackie

From: sara@e-mail.com

To: jackie@e-mail.com

Sent: 3 February

Subject: A lazy trainee

Jackie

Thanks for your e-mail about my potentially lazy participant. I think I need to talk to him, but I'm not sure how to approach him. Last time I spoke to someone in this way, we ended up arguing – 'No, I don't...' 'Yes, you do!'. Any ideas how to avoid the row?

Sara

From:	jackie@e-mail.com
To:	sara@e-mail.com
Sent:	14 February
Subject:	A lazy trainee

Dear Sara

I think that you need to think of that well-known phrase 'Be prepared'!

Imagine you are the other person and consider 'How would I want to be approached?'. The answer to this question will undoubtedly be 'with sensitivity and in private'.

Consider what you want to get from the conversation. From your first message I imagine that you want to find out why the person seems to be avoiding situations in the training room and whether you can do anything to address the reasons.

Plan your opening statement and finish it with a question. I suggest that you point out to the person what it is that they are doing that is causing you a problem. This is what I did with the person that I mentioned to you in my first reply: 'I notice that you seem to be missing at the start of every group activity, is there a problem?'. As I said to you, I got a negative response at first, and I think this was because I used a closed question rather than an open one. You might want to try something like 'I am wondering why you seem to be missing at the start of every group activity,' asked with a questioning tone to your voice.

Take the participant to a private area where you can't be overheard and ask your question. Then it's important not to say anything else. Even if the person doesn't immediately answer, the silence will probably be enough to get them to talk to you.

I hope the trainee will start to explain the problem at this point. If he doesn't, you'll have to insist on an explanation. You can do this by pointing out the effect his absences are having on the success of the activities and on the other members of the group. Even though you're becoming more insistent, you should still ensure that the person knows that you're sensitive by using appropriate tone and body language. I know you're very good at listening. ...

Cont.

... Once you've used your questioning and listening to get to the bottom of the problem, you'll need to start looking for solutions. Explain to the person that you value his input to the group and that you don't want to lose him from the course. Point out some of the ways he's added to the learning of the other participants. Then go on to ask, 'What can be done to resolve this situation? How can we make you feel more at ease in the group situations?'. At this point you should be able to negotiate some joint solutions to the problem – you'll need to make sure that the solutions will not only work for your participant, but also for you as the trainer and group leader.

Sara, remember that this process may not be successful. You may have a person who is not ready to discuss the reasons behind his behaviour and you're not a counsellor, you have responsibilities to the whole group not simply to the single participant. If you can't reach a workable solution, then you'll need to explain to the participant that he'll have to find other ways of learning this particular topic. Then you'll need to discuss the situation with his manager. (This is a last resort.)

Good luck.

Jackie

From:	sara@e-mail.com
To:	jackie@e-mail.com
Sent:	15 February
Subject:	A lazy trainee

Dear Jackie

I think I copped out! I thought about talking to the guy, and usually I would just confront the behaviour. However, during the coffee break, I asked him if everything was OK and he said 'Yes'. Not the answer I wanted! So, when I was briefing the next task, I broke them into two groups, and said that he and someone from the other group were going to be group leaders, and that they had to come to me for the briefing. (This way he couldn't miss the start of the activity.) He didn't seem very happy, and actually the group didn't do the task very well.

I thought the issue was solved as the group discussed the importance of having a clear brief and spending time ensuring that everyone understood what was required of them at the start of the task.

For the next exercise, he reverted to his normal behaviour! No, I didn't address it! I decided it was in the 'too-hard pile'.

Yours – a coward!
Sara

From: sara@e-mail.com

To: jackie@e-mail.com

Sent: 15 February

Subject: Help!

Dear Jackie

Have you got any ideas for dealing with equipment failure? I'm currently involved in showing staff how to use a new piece of machinery, but it keeps breaking down. I've rung maintenance and they come out and do what they can, but the machinery just breaks down again. Also, if they're busy dealing with other production issues, it takes a long time for them to come to us.

The whole point is that this machine is going to do away with some of the manual work, and make life easier. However, I think the staff see the machine as being unreliable and more of a nuisance than something worth having. Also the training is a little bit of a waste of time – I can't show them how to use a machine that doesn't work.

I've got three issues:

I can't run the session the way it's written and I don't know what other relevant things to do with the group.

The participants think the machine doesn't work properly.

I'm embarrassed!

Any ideas about what I can do?

Sara

E-mail 40

From: jackie@e-mail.com

To: sara@e-mail.com

Sent: 22 October

Subject: Help!

Sara

What a problem; I sympathize wholeheartedly with you. Here are a few ideas, however, I think the main thing to do is to impress upon your maintenance team that you need priority – after all, if no one knows how to use the machine, there's not much point having it, is there?

Do you know why your machine keeps breaking down and does this happen with the other ones in the company? Perhaps you could get a technical person to explain the issues to your trainees – or if this is not possible, the technician could draft a memo, which you could give out as a handout.

If, however, you have to wait for the machine to be fixed, you might want to try the following training ideas:

- What about training some coaches in the live environment and have your trainees work alongside them (on-the-job training)? For now perhaps you could act as coach yourself. Are there any spare machines to use for training in the live environment? And can you identify some non-urgent work for trainees to do as part of their on-the-job training? Is there a process for rectifying their mistakes if they train 'in live'?
- Could you create exercises where the trainees see on paper what the machine does and how it works? (These might include giving them cards describing the machine's functions to put into the right order, and/or identifying what input/output comes from each stage.)
- Could you go through some exercises using the training machine and a video camera, then play it in class if the machine breaks down?
- Could you design a computer-based learning package? I don't know how to do it exactly but with all the technology that's around, you should be able to simulate how the machine works.

This is a very difficult situation and, as I've said, I really do feel that the root of it needs to be addressed. Good luck and let me know how you get on.

Regards
Jackie

From:	sara@e-mail.com
To:	jackie@e-mail.com
Sent:	29 October
Subject:	Help!

Dear Jackie

The machine is still a problem! My manager says that he is now meeting every two weeks with maintenance to discuss the issues. I've asked if I could go to some of the meetings and we've agreed that I will go to the next one if things don't improve.

Meanwhile, I've tried a couple of your ideas. They've been quite successful so thought you might like the feedback.

I found your idea about linking with 'live' interesting and have spent some time discussing it with the team leaders. We agreed that they probably didn't have the either the time or the skill set to take on more on-the-job training at the moment. However, last time the machine stopped working, I took a group down to 'live' and helped them process real work. This was a great idea as they were towards the end of their training, so it really helped them transfer the new skills and understand what the new processes would be. It also helped me, as I was able to check that I was doing it the same way as they do in the operation. The team leaders were happy that we'd processed some work as well! I think I'll do this again, but only with people who are almost ready to go back to work.

I developed your idea of the cards – I drew pictures of the control panel on to a flipchart then had it laminated. Participants have to indicate which control they would use for different functions. This means we can still get familiar with the panel without being on the machine.

Using these methods coupled with quizzes and discussions is getting us through the course with fewer gaps.

Thanks.

Sara

From: jackie@e-mail.com

To: sara@e-mail.com

Sent: 30 February

Subject: I'm an anorak!

Sara

You're going to think I'm a real anorak, but I've just realized how much what you've been doing relates to all the theories of training and learning that we have talked about over the years!

It seems to me that your machine failure gave you an opportunity to appeal to all the different learning styles within the group:

- The activists got to do something – they were able to visit the 'real world' and you gave them other classroom-based activities to do.
- The reflectors had time to think about what they had done in the training room and then consider how they would apply it in the workplace. The activity with the laminated flipcharts also gave them the chance to reflect on what they'd covered during the sessions.
- The theorists had the chance to think about the control panels, their functions and how everything fits together. They also had the chance to look at the live environment and to work out how their part of the process fits into the operation as a whole.
- The pragmatists were able to see the live environment and to put into practice what they had learnt in the classroom.

Another thing is that you used a variety of methods to help reinforce the learning. This made it more likely that the participants had learnt at various levels, which would help with memory recall.

You also put participants under some real pressure in the live environment, which would have made them concentrate on applying their learning. Because you were then able to return to the training environment, they had the opportunity to consider the problems that they might encounter in the real world and how these might be overcome.

The other benefit is that the managers were able to see how you work and that you take the training of their staff very seriously.

It's amazing how a disaster can become a triumph!

Jackie

From: jackie@e-mail.com

To: sara@e-mail.com

Sent: 25 September

Subject: Lost inspiration

Sara, hello again...

I was wondering if you'd be able to help me with this little question. I know that you've done all sorts of different activities in your time and I remember you saying that we should always look for the most creative solution. I think my creativity has packed its bags today!

A manager has approached me about three people in his area who are having problems with the teams that report to them. Apparently they can't get the employees to do the work they're being asked to do. The manager in question has asked me to book or run an assertiveness course.

Having both delivered and attended courses on assertiveness, I'm not sure that a course is the best way to get these people to learn this skill. I'm also concerned because I know that these three people are very practical and will probably not be happy in a classroom situation.

How can I be creative in this situation? I know that I can run a course, but I don't think this will help. I would really appreciate your comments on this one.

Jackie

From:	sara@e-mail.com
To:	jackie@e-mail.com
Sent:	25 September
Subject:	Creativity

Hi!

If you don't want to run a course, why don't you try out some 'lunch and shares'. These are workshops where people come along and talk about their experiences. They're great ways of getting them to learn from each other.

Alternatively, have you got any self-learning or distance-learning information they could use? Last year I lent some videos to one of the managers. She showed them in her team meeting and encouraged a discussion. This worked well, because one of her people would not admit to needing training.

Hope this helps.

Regards
Sara

From: jackie@e-mail.com

To: sara@e-mail.com

Sent: 11 October

Subject: Wow!

Sara

Just wanted to tell you what a star you are and how much your suggestions on what to do instead of running a course have taken off.

The first thing that I did was to invite the manager and his team leaders to a lunchtime gathering. I had informal meetings with team leaders and the manager to make the invitation. We discussed with each person the situation that they're facing with their team and suggested that we all get together to discuss how they might handle things differently. I was really pleased when all the team leaders jumped at the chance to get together.

During the lunchtime session we discussed reasons why the team leaders might be struggling with their teams and we all had an opportunity to discuss ways forward.

I gave each person a questionnaire with a series of questions designed to get them thinking about the way they lead their team. I also gave them some 'diary' sheets on which they were to make notes about each situation where they have a problem with their team. We agreed to meet again in three weeks' time to review the situation. For the meantime I suggested some reading for them and pointed them in the direction of a video on team leadership that's in our library.

Three weeks later we got together again over lunch with their manager present, to discuss what had been happening. I was hugely impressed that not only had the three team leaders completed the questionnaire and the diary, but also the manager, *and* they had all watched the video and done the reading! The discussions at this get-together centred on the diaries and how much each person had started to realize what he or she was doing that inhibited their team leadership skills. Even the manager had some thoughts about ways in which he could improve. Each person had different issues at the top of their priority list – one wanted to work on effective delegation, ...

… another on verbal communication and the last on forward planning. The manager had recognized his role in team development and had realized how little support he had given the team leaders since they had taken on their new role.

I really can't believe that a simple lunch and a huge dose of motivation can produce such exciting results.

All I can say is 'Thank you' and I'm glad I didn't run the assertiveness course straight away – I was assertive enough to say 'No' to the manager!

See you next week at the conference I hope.

Jackie

From:	jackie@e-mail.com
To:	sara@e-mail.com
Sent:	28 February
Subject:	Being creative

Sara

Help! I have to do a workshop on report writing. The last time I ran the course that we usually use everyone was almost asleep by the end of the first session and that included me! It was SO boring.

What do you think that I could do to spice it up a bit? (Bear in mind that the delegates come from a department where they are encouraged to be very conservative and refined!)

Jackie

From: sara@e-mail.com

To: jackie@e-mail.com

Sent: 28 February

Subject: Being creative

Jackie

Have you got any practical sessions built into the day?

If you want to spice up the input or plenary sessions, try and get them to find the answers for themselves. The following are good ways of doing that: In groups, on flipchart, list…

Debate a subject, eg 'This house believes that all reports should have an executive summary as the front page' or 'This house believes that written reports are unnecessary'. Split into two groups and get them to prepare two speakers for the debate, one for, and one against.

Activities aimed at improving proof-reading can be fun, eg spot how many times the letter 's' appears in a paragraph.

Give each participant a different sentence on a piece of card, put them into small groups and make them write a report on a given subject that includes these sentences – the subjects can be very obscure.

Ask them to bring a report with them or provide some yourself and get them to critique in small groups and share in plenary.

That's all I can think of at the moment.

Sara

From: sara@e-mail.com

To: jackie@e-mail.com

Sent: 2 December

Subject: Questions, questions and more questions...

Hi there!

I had one particularly challenging person in my group today – he never stopped asking questions! He started with questions about the arrangements for the day, then he asked about the pre-course work, then about the theories behind the input that I was presenting and every time I set an exercise or activity he asked for clarification. The other participants appeared to be quite frustrated with him – as was I! I tried my most assertive 'Thank you for your question, but I'd like to hear from someone else', but it had no effect.

He's back in my group next week and I've got a feeling that if I don't do something the others will walk out!

I'd appreciate some ideas if you have any.

Thanks.

Sara

From:	jackie@e-mail.com
To:	sara@e-mail.com
Sent:	2 December
Subject:	Questions...

Sara

This is a bit of a tough one since you tried the things I would normally suggest.

I wonder if it would be possible to contact this person prior to the next session and arrange to have an informal meeting. During the meeting say that you're a little concerned about the number of questions he was asking at the last session and you'd like to clarify any points that he may have misunderstood. Explain that you're happy to deal with questions as they arise, however, so many questions coming from the same person can be disruptive. Ask him how he would feel is he were one of the other delegates. Also ask him if there's anything you could do to make the session fit his needs more closely, but explain that by focusing your attention on him, it may appear to the others that you are favouring only one person and that this would not be fair.

Another alternative, if you're unable to meet, would be to draw attention to the evaluation forms that you received at the end of the last session. You could say that a recurring comment was that you strayed from the topic too often throughout the session (which may or may not have been a written comment – if it was, then fine – if it wasn't then how do you feel about telling a white lie?). You could go on to say that you have decided to have a 'car park' this week so that if a question arises that is not directly related to the subject at hand, you will park it on the car park flipchart and it will be addressed at the end of the session or on an individual basis. Even if you don't refer to the evaluation forms, you could still use the car park strategy by saying that you're aware of the lack of focus in the previous session and want to make sure that you keep to the point this time.

You may also wish to reiterate (or add to) your ground rules. If you have a rule about 'do not monopolize the discussion' you could refer to this one when your questioner gets going. ...

> **Cont.**
>
> ... I suppose that your final option would be to simply say to the person that, whilst questions are good, not all the answers come from the trainer and it would be very good to make sure that he listens to other people in the group. In order to do that he may have to bite his tongue before he asks the next question. You know that he is an intelligent person and quite often, if he takes time to reflect on what is being said, he will come up with the answers for himself. 'God gave us one mouth and two ears; use them in that proportion.'
>
> Hope this helps – let me know how you get on and whether any of these ideas work!
>
> Jackie

From: sara@e-mail.com

To: jackie@e-mail.com

Sent: 8 December

Subject: My questioner

I met my questioner in the queue in the canteen earlier this week. After the usual 'Hi, how are you?' he asked me if I was happy with the course. Another question! I said I thought it'd been OK but that really I should be asking him and the others that. He said he thought the course was great and that he'd got loads out of it.

At this point, I asked him to share a table with me, thinking that this could be a good time to explore my issue with his behaviour. The conversation went something like this:

Me: 'I'm glad you found the course useful – what did you specifically like about it?'.

Him: 'You were so helpful and willing to answer my questions. I also liked being able to discuss things with other people – in my team you get into trouble if you ask for information. You're supposed to just get on with your job'.

Me (light dawning!): 'It sounds as if you sometimes find that frustrating'.

Him: 'Yes, I do. I like to know what is happening and why'.

Me: 'Is that why you asked so many questions on the course?'.

Him: 'Did I ask too many? – I won't say anything next time if that's the case'.

Me: 'I didn't mean that. I was concerned that I wasn't giving you enough information – I certainly don't want to you to stop asking relevant questions. It's just that sometimes, I felt as if you were asking me questions for the sake of it'.

Anyway, he was not happy and said he didn't know what I meant – was he to ask questions or not? We agreed that he could carry on as usual and I would ...

... try and make sure that I explained everything fully, but if he asked too many questions I would tell him at the time.

Today, he was in my group, and he started off being very quiet and not really joining in with discussions. I asked him at the break if he was OK and he said he was – but he was just trying not to ask too many questions!

I ended up saying that I rather he asked lots of questions than not join in at all!

So, the outcome is that he asked questions, some I answered, some I said 'I'll answer that after the exercise', and others I said 'What do you think?'. Overall, I'm not happy with the end result, but I'll see how it goes in the next module!

Regards
Sara

From: jackie@e-mail.com

To: sara@e-mail.com

Sent: 25 January

Subject: The real need

Sara

I hope you'll be able to offer some advice on this one – I know from previous communication that you have been doing a full training needs analysis recently and I would value your experience. If you could get back to me within the next few hours it would be good since I have a meeting with the manager of the department first thing tomorrow!

Last week one of our senior managers asked me to run a course on delegation for a group of first-line managers. I thought I asked all the right questions, such as why do you feel this training is required, what tells you that these managers are having problems with delegation and so on. The senior manager told me that his managers are telling him they can't cope with their workloads. To him they seem to be working very hard – they're all in the office for many more hours than their contract requires – but they don't seem to be achieving the required results. The manager has had a number of complaints about unanswered e-mails and non-returned voicemail messages. When he has tackled the individuals involved they've told him that they've been so busy working through the pile of paperwork and messages on their desk that they haven't had time to return calls or answer e-mails. They've also told him that they haven't always got the information they need to respond. To me this sounded like a classic case of poor delegation skills.

Then I had the following experience which made me think again…

I overheard a conversation in the canteen between two of the potential delegates. They were talking about the fact that they haven't managed to keep any administrative and clerical staff in the department for longer than three months. This has resulted in a huge backlog of filing and paperwork. They also said that no one in the department is really clear on what is expected of them and who is supposed to be responsible for what. I'm beginning to suspect that a course on delegation won't help. It seems to me …

... that there's a problem stemming from the way in which the department is structured and the way work is allocated.

What do you think that I should do next? Should I go ahead with the course and risk real backlash from the delegates? Should I use the course to find out what is really going on and then report back? Or should I tell the senior manager what I have heard when I meet him tomorrow morning?

I need some advice – you won't let me down will you???

Jackie

From:	sara@e-mail.com
To:	jackie@e-mail.com
Sent:	25 January
Subject:	The real need

Dear Jackie

Situations like this rarely have only one cause, ie lack of skills. It sounds like there are several problems facing the department – the trick is to help the manager to take a multi-pronged approach. Sometimes it's very easy for us as trainers to think our courses are the solution to everything. The one thing I have learnt over the past year is that it's our role to help everyone develop, and I'm increasingly seeing the importance of coaching and supporting line managers 'in the field' as part of achieving our learning and organizational objectives.

So: you have a manager who has asked for your help – he wants you to run a skills course, which may help but not completely solve the issues. You have participants who are unhappy with aspects of their organization, but who are not (for whatever reason) communicating with their line manager to resolve the problems. You don't want to run a course that won't meet the participants' needs and equally I'm assuming you don't want to lose the opportunity to work with the team.

Use your meeting tomorrow as an opportunity to help the manager identify the true needs. I would start by recapping what he's told you about the needs, and saying that you agree with him that a delegation course may be beneficial.

I don't think that you should directly mention the overheard conversation. Explain that you'd like his help to ensure that the course really meets the needs of his staff and achieves his objective of improving performance. You'd like to discuss the needs in greater detail with him which will also help your understanding of the day-to-day situation facing the participants. Then ask questions like:

When we train delegation skills, we talk a lot about having clear roles, responsibilities and objectives – this helps us to identify what can and ...

… cannot be delegated – as well as prioritize tasks. How well do you think that your line managers will be able to do this?

Are we likely to be told that there is no point in delegating because there is no one to delegate to?

After the training, what support will participants get in using their new skills? What is likely to help them? What is likely to hinder them?

Depending upon his answers, you should be in a position to suggest a two-phased approach – a workshop with him and the managers about the organization, covering roles and responsibilities, followed by the course on delegation.

You might also consider asking him if you could meet with the delegates, either individually or as a group, prior to designing the day. You can then give them a structured needs questionnaire which you could use with him to decide upon the content of the course. This way you'll know precisely what the needs are.

Good luck tomorrow!

Regards
Sara

From: sara@e-mail.com

To: jackie@e-mail.com

Sent: 28 January

Subject: The real need

Dear Jackie

In your e-mail of 25 January you referred to the training needs analysis I've been doing. Well, now I've finished and I thought that you might be interested in hearing about it.

We decided to use a two-pronged approach – a review of the corporate business plans and structured interviews with the department managers. At the same time, I wanted to use this as an opportunity for the managers to give me feedback on the service they receive from our department. A copy of the questionnaire we used is attached. (*Dear Reader – see Action points for a form similar to the one described here.*)

Overall, the approach worked and I have lots of information, which I'm currently using to build an annual training calendar for the company. It also provided me with the opportunity to meet with line managers who I seldom see, to talk about how we can support them. So the advantages of doing this analysis, for me, have been:

- Lots of information about what training is needed to achieve business objectives next year.
- Clear explanations about why managers request certain courses.
- Opportunity to rectify some misunderstandings about what training is and how I can help the line managers.
- Greater understanding of how departments work and the issues that might affect them achieving their training plans, such as: weeks to avoid because of workloads, major deadlines, organizational and resource issues.
- Better relationships on an individual basis with line managers.
- A corporate training calendar for the next 12 months.
- Individual department training plans, which can be reviewed at quarterly meetings. ...

Cont.

… It wasn't all easy going though!

Getting some of the managers to meet with me and discuss training took some patience – one of them stood me up three times!

Halfway through, I got really concerned about the lack of clear priorities – if managers don't know their priorities, what chance have their staff? However, I intend to feed this into the management development programme, and have spoken to some of the directors about how to increase awareness generally.

Another disadvantage of handling training needs analysis this way is that it's quite time-consuming.

All in all, I will do this again as I think that the benefits outweigh the disadvantages. Keep in touch, I would be interested in your experiences.

Sara

From: sara@e-mail.com

To: jackie@e-mail.com

Sent: 31 January

Subject: Training needs analysis

Hi

I've just finished the training needs analysis report but I'm not sure about the best way to present it to the board and senior managers. I've got loads of information, but not all of it is strictly about training needs. Some of the comments are about lack of resources or involve the company values and culture.

Any thoughts on ways of presenting this so that the senior managers hear what I have to tell them? My fear is they'll just ignore the wider messages, or get so involved with them that they'll gloss over the training plans.

Sara

From:	jackie@e-mail.com
To:	sara@e-mail.com
Sent:	1 February
Subject:	Training needs analysis

Sara

I can reply from bitter experience! In my last job, following a training needs analysis, I was involved in presenting a report to senior mangers. The report gave all the facts in plain and direct terms. Afterwards I was told to 'stop poking my nose in where it was not wanted'! I sensed I may have touched a raw nerve!

After this experience, I'd suggest diplomacy and tact are key. Remember that you want to keep these people on your side and not leave them feeling as if they've been attacked. I think the first thing to do, if possible, is to talk through your findings with someone you trust to help you decide the priorities; decide which findings need to be highlighted in the report; which require a one-on-one with individual line managers; and which you can disregard.

If you don't have anyone to talk through your findings with, the next best thing could be listing them and the evidence for each one. Doing this might show you that some of your thoughts are based simply on gut reaction and whilst this is valid, managers will also be looking for some proof in order to make business decisions.

Once you've gone through all your findings, divide the issues into training needs and other needs. Since managers will want you to come to them with 'solutions not problems', your reporting will be seen as being very constructive because you've considered different ways in which each need could be addressed.

The other thing to remember is that managers won't want any surprises. If you have to make a presentation to a group of managers, I'd suggest meeting each one informally before the presentation so they're prepared to respond to what you have to say. ...

Cont.

… In summary, I think your course of action should be:

- List the needs that have arisen from the meetings and prioritize them.
- Categorize the needs into training and other needs.
- Consider ways in which the needs may be addressed.
- Prepare a concise, constructive and positive report. Focus on the evidence you've collected.
- Discuss your findings on an individual basis with managers.
- Prepare a presentation focusing on what can be done, a plan to do it, and how much it will cost.

I hope this helps.

Regards
Jackie

From: sara@e-mail.com

To: jackie@e-mail.com

Sent: 1 March

Subject: Training needs analysis

Dear Jackie

I've just finished presenting the training needs analysis to the Board, and it seems to have gone well. I took some of your advice and wrote down all the issues and needs. They fell into three categories:

- Training needs. These were included in the training plans and calendars.
- Localized issues. I have met separately with three line mangers about these.
- Issues that are company-wide but aren't really training needs. I took the two biggest of these and included them at the end of my presentation under the heading 'factors that might adversely affect training'.

This way the presentation could focus solely on the training needs and solutions. The board were happy to agree the plans I'd made. I've said I'll meet with department heads in six months' time to review the plan and make sure it's still correct.

Thanks.

Sara

From:	sara@e-mail.com
To:	jackie@e-mail.com
Sent:	5 March
Subject:	It's only a game!

Dear Jackie

Quote of the year: 'It's only a Lego game'.

There's someone on my personal skill development programme who constantly cracks jokes. I thought it was quite funny at first but now, halfway through the programme, it's getting on my nerves. It doesn't matter what we're doing – group discussions, exercises, working in pairs, or whatever – he's in entertaining mode.

Today, as part of building effective teams, I included the Lego tower activity. He was very 'playful' and kept knocking down the tower or using the bricks to build a plane. Two of the others in his group were really annoyed at him as it meant they couldn't achieve the task. As part of the debrief, I asked him why, and he said: 'It's only a Lego game, you've got to have a laugh'.

When he first joined the group I thought he would be good, as he was friendly and outgoing. Now I'm concerned that not only is he not taking the training seriously, but also his behaviour is distracting for others. The next module is in two weeks – should I ignore this problem?

Sara

From: jackie@e-mail.com

To: sara@e-mail.com

Sent: 6 March

Subject: It's only a game!

Sara

Firstly, I have to admire you for keeping your patience with this person. He sounds incredibly annoying. I wonder what the real reasons are behind his behaviour? Does he participate productively between his bouts of joking? When you ask direct questions, or for feedback, does he ever answer?

I'm no psychologist, but I wonder if this is the way he was at school and whether being in the training room causes him to revert to his classroom behaviour?

I don't think that ignoring this particular problem will make it go away. I'd say you need to tackle it head on. It's obviously not simply a personality clash between you and the delegate since you say that other participants are showing their annoyance at his behaviour.

Either prior to the next session or during the very first coffee break, I suggest you take him aside to talk about his behaviour. Describe exactly what he's doing and the reaction it provokes from you and the other delegates. Explain to him that you like to have a laugh as much as the next person and that learning should be fun, however his behaviour is starting to make you wonder if he's learning anything at all from the programme. Make it clear to him what you would like to happen – that is, have fun, but do not distract others through continuous joking – and let him know that if it continues you'll ask him to stop whenever it's becoming too much.

The underlying process to this is:

• Tell him what he's doing.
• Explain the consequences of his behaviour.
• Tell him what you'd like him to do and the way in which you expect him to behave.
• Explain the consequences of him not behaving in a more appropriate way. ...

... This may sound a bit like dealing with a naughty child, and in some ways I suppose it is. Therefore you'll need to be careful not to get into the parent–child mode. Make sure you deal with this situation adult-to-adult and that you don't become patronizing and like a schoolteacher. If you feel this is happening, then there's no harm in acknowledging it, apologizing and then going back to explaining your point.

Talk to him about what he hopes to gain from the training and whether he feels he's succeeding. Discuss with him the different ways in which people learn and ask him how he has learnt the best in the past.

You may find that by talking to him you uncover some underlying insecurities and if you and he feel comfortable enough, you may wish to discuss them with him in a one-to-one meeting. It may even be that he has some learning difficulty and is trying to cover it up with his joking.

If you find that there is no underlying problem, or if he's not willing to discuss the situation with you and the joking carries on, you'll have no alternative but to remove him from the group.

Hope these ideas solve your problem – I'll be interested to hear what you find out.

All the best
Jackie

From: sara@e-mail.com

To: jackie@e-mail.com

Sent: 10 March

Subject: It's only a game!

Jackie

I spoke to my joker. I was fully prepared for all sorts of possible directions the conversation might take after reading your advice. The short answer as to why this guy was behaving like this is that he just thought he was funny!

We've agreed that in future if I think it's getting too much I will give him feedback there and then.

Thanks for the advice.

Sara

From:	sara@e-mail.com
To:	jackie@e-mail.com
Sent:	15 March
Subject:	Ideas for activities

Hi Jackie

I've just finished designing a leadership day and when I read through the material I realized that there's a lot of me talking to them. I've included a brainstorm and some OHP slides, but I want to include some practical exercises such as building Lego towers. I'm concerned after my experience with the joker, but also because one of the personnel officers said that they hated being made to do 'childish exercises' on courses.

How can I pick good exercises that people will want to do? I don't want them to think that they are just games!

Sara

From: jackie@e-mail.com

To: sara@e-mail.com

Sent: 16 March

Subject: Ideas for activities

Good morning to you.

I know how you feel – and I've had a number of people saying that 'all these games are just a waste of time'. The comforting thing is that once the people do start to participate, they actually get something out of them.

One of the tactics I've used in the past is to not tell people that there will be 'fun' activities. On the course outline I simply write 'team-building task' and leave them to make their own minds up. I think that you need to be sure in your own mind why you're including the activity. If you have clear objectives and you can explain to the participants how the activity fulfils these you can be quite comfortable about using even the silliest of things.

If you feel that this would really be inappropriate for your group then what I suggest you do is to look at the Lego activity and see if you can make it more relevant. Perhaps you could replace the Lego with items from your engineering workshop or with other company-related objects.

There are several activities on the market that can be adapted to specific organizations. I used the following recently with a group of team leaders (they were all quite cynical at first, but they did respond after we discussed the learning points from the activity):

Split your participants into groups of three or four. Explain that they have been asked to design a model that will be given out to delegates at the international trade fair next month. The main objective is that the item must be economical to produce and that it must represent the company in some way. They must work together to produce the model. They're allowed to use whatever equipment you provide them with, anything extra they use will cost £x. Have sticky labels, cardboard tubes, boxes, string, etc to hand out along with a price list. ...

... You set the time limit. I gave my groups 20 minutes to plan and 20 minutes to construct. At the end of the working time, each group must present its model, the rationale behind the model and a costing.

The important thing with any activity like this is the debriefing process. You'll need to decide what you wanted the participants to learn and then have them discuss a set of relevant questions such as: Who took the lead? How was the work allocated? Did all members of the team contribute?

Hope this helps. I will say again – if you have the objectives and you know that the activity will work towards their achievement, you'll be able to sell to the group.

Have fun.

Jackie

From:	jackie@e-mail.com
To:	sara@e-mail.com
Sent:	1 September
Subject:	Equal opportunities

Dear Sara

My organization is in the midst of writing an equal opportunities policy and procedure manual. The policy and manual will cover all aspects of HR (recruitment, selection, training, etc) and also working practices.

I've been asked to write the piece for the policy and manual on training. I've managed to put together a paragraph for the policy which covers issues such as access to training programmes for all regardless of race, disability, religion and sex. It also states that our programmes will be designed in such a way so as to respond to different learning styles and needs – ie we will look at a variety of ways to cover the same material.

I'm now looking at the piece for the procedure manual. I've written a little about the variety of learning methods and now I want to write something about how we'll work in classroom-based sessions in order that all group members have the same opportunities to learn. I want to say something about ground rules and I wondered what types of ground rules you use when you're running a session to cover this area.

Can you come back to me as soon as possible as I have to have this written by the end of the week. Sorry about the pressure!

Jackie

From: sara@e-mail.com

To: jackie@e-mail.com

Sent: 2 February

Subject: Equal opportunities/ground rules

Dear Jackie

To be honest, I really only ever suggest ground rules covering three areas. They are:

- Mutual respect. Everyone will treat everyone else how they like to be treated themselves; people will listen to others and not interrupt or trivialize other's comments.
- Honesty and confidentiality. People will not tell others who said what or repeat specific examples. This allows everyone to be honest and open, and to share his or her ideas.
- Full participation. Everyone will participate fully in the course, whatever that means for them.

I then allow the group to add any ground rules of their own (and they usually come out with rules about breaks and smoking).

I've recently been training with a company that has some quite good ground rules relating to how their staff work with individuals, but you could turn them into course ground rules. (These are reproduced with the permission of Emphasis Training):

- Treat each participant as an individual who has a valuable contribution to make.
- Plan practical activities in order to give each participant an opportunity to practise the skills and apply the relevant knowledge.
- Be supportive in communicating with individuals.
- Challenge the thinking of individuals in a supportive environment.

Regards
Sara

From: jackie@e-mail.com

To: sara@e-mail.com

Sent: 1 July

Subject: How to use pre- and post-course work

Sara

Do you use pre- and post-course work when you're running training courses? Does it work? Can you get the delegates to complete it? The reason I ask is that I'm running a workshop for a group of team leaders next month. I want to have the delegates thinking in advance about some of the issues we'll be covering. I want them to complete a learning styles questionnaire and a Belbin Team Roles Inventory, but I'm wondering how many questionnaires and articles I should send out with the joining instructions. I also want them to do some reading about action-centred leadership and team building. I know that they're all busy people and that their managers won't allow them much time for 'homework'. I also know that the last time I did this, half the group forgot to bring their completed pre-course work with them!

The other thing I want to do is give some post-course work so that the participants can keep on learning after the course has finished. My concern is that people won't have the time or the support needed to complete the work.

What do you think I should do?

Jackie

From:	sara@e-mail.com
To:	jackie@e-mail.com
Sent:	3 July
Subject:	How to use pre- and post-course work

Jackie

Yes, I have used pre- and post-course work for some of the programmes we run, and I've had similar experiences to the ones you describe! The one which sticks out in my mind the most involved a management course which is four modules run over six months.

On the first module, we sent out a questionnaire for participants to complete and bring with them, the intention being to review the answers whilst discussing the underpinning theory. Out of the nine participants, four hadn't completed the questionnaire. We took a break to allow them time to do it, which meant we finished at 6.30 pm instead of 6 pm. I also took time out to explain to the group the reason why we give pre-course work and the importance of completing it. After a short discussion, we agreed to include it as a ground rule as a sub-section of 'full participation'.

I've used pre-course work on other courses such as time management, but I try to limit it to no more than 30–60 minutes' work, and I always explain why it's required and how it links to the training session. Also, I include it in my introduction to the session: 'You were asked to do this and we will be discussing/using it after the break'. If the necessary task won't take long, those who haven't done it should be able to do so in their break, or they'll tell you they haven't done it, which allows you some time to think about re-ordering things.

It's harder to know what goes on with post-course work. If I'm seeing a group again, as in the above programme, I set post-course work and tell them that we'll begin the next module with them sharing their experiences with the group, via a presentation or discussion. However, if the course is a one-off, it's hard to know whether they really do the work or not. In theory, post-course work is an excellent way of getting them to put their learning into practice, but in the real world... A classic example of this is action planning resulting from a training course – how often have we drawn up a plan on a course, put it in our folders and ignored it? ...

> ### Cont.
>
> ... If I do set post-course work, I e-mail the participants' line managers after the course to let them know and make a clear request for them to support the participant. There is a section on our evaluation forms which says 'Has the post-course work been completed? How successful was it?'. The evaluation form is sent to the line manger and the correct procedure is that the participant and the line manager fill it in together.
>
> Another technique is to send participants a reminder about the post-course work three weeks after the training. This reminder might include a copy of the action plan they completed during the course.
>
> Sara

From:	sara@e-mail.com
To:	jackie@e-mail.com
Sent:	27 July
Subject:	How to use pre- and post-course work

Dear Jackie

How are you getting on with the use of pre- and post-course work?

I've just used it successfully as part of our Health and Safety training course. Not only were we able to reduce the course length, we also avoided having to stand up and deliver the boring legal bit!

We sent out two pieces of work:

• Reading material on the Health and Safety at Work Act, and the Company Policy Document.
• A pro-forma which participants had to fill in prior to coming on the course, by walking around their offices and identifying things that fulfilled legal and policy requirements, and things that were potential hazards.

I was surprised that this seemed to capture the minds of our participants, all of whom came with the pro-forma filled in. We had a very useful discussion about why things were hazards and whose responsibility it was to ensure that they were dealt with.

I'm intending to send the pro-formas back to them as post-course work and to ask them to see if the hazards are still there. They'll be asked to then forward the pro-forma to the premises manager so that he gets feedback on the real situation.

The workshop is scheduled to run again next week; I am actually looking forward to it!

Sara

From: sara@e-mail.com

To: jackie@e-mail.com

Sent: 31 July

Subject: The moaners

Dear Jackie

I've probably had one of my worst courses since coming back to training full time!

I was training a group of managers, some of whom have been in their positions for quite a while, whilst the others are fairly new to their jobs. The first session last month was 'What is management?', moving on to the role and responsibilities of a manager. All I got for the entire morning was complaints – how badly they were managed, how it was all so good in theory but the company doesn't work like that, how they don't get time to spend time with their staff, etc etc. We spent quite a lot of time discussing these issues, as they seemed so important to the participants. I worked really hard to get them to agree that whether they were performing as managers or not, they should be; and that their action plans should show how they could spend time doing their jobs!

Today is Session 2 on performance management. This is a standard course about setting standards and expectations, measuring performance and giving feedback. Well, it's now lunchtime and I think I'm losing it! Two of the participants have spent the whole morning moaning – they can't do the things we were talking about because their managers wouldn't like it, they're not allowed to, it doesn't really work that way in their departments, etc etc. It felt like a re-run of the last session, only worse! They were moaning about how demotivated staff were, but couldn't see that they are responsible as managers to run their teams and overcome their own and other managers' past mistakes!

We are due back in an hour and I really don't know what to do – any ideas?

Yours desperately
Sara

E-mail 68

From:	jackie@e-mail.com
To:	sara@e-mail.com
Sent:	31 July
Subject:	The moaners

Oh dear! Sara, this is probably one of the hardest situations to deal with. You've given participants an opportunity to voice their issues, but it sounds like they are not actually moving on from those issues, or taking responsibility to make them better! Perhaps the areas you're covering threaten them, and rather than try out ideas, they're blocking them straight away.

I've had participants in the past who've made excuses about why they can't implement the learning – often these involve other people or the company. In reality, they're scared of change or haven't really accepted that change is necessary.

We can discuss later the theories about why people do these things, but in the meantime, here are some ideas for you to try this afternoon:

- The participants moan, ask them to park those issues until you get to the action planning stage. Tell them you'll discuss the issues then as part of how they will implement their learning, what will help them and what won't.
- When you go back after lunch, give the group a choice. Say you're concerned that a number of company issues keep coming up, such as: staff motivation, empowerment, etc, and that they seem to be detracting from the main objectives of the programme. Tell them that you'd like to give the group two options: either to carry on with the course as planned, and put the other issues aside as they are unlikely to get solved as part of the course; or to stop the course, and spend the rest of the time talking about the wider issues and what the participants can do about them. If the participants chose the latter, they have to be willing to find solutions and not just moan. This way, the group can decide its priority. The majority wish wins.
- Tell the two people to shut up! Nicely, of course.

I think whatever you do you need to talk to these participants' line managers about the different issues coming up, so that the managers can do something about them.

Hope this helps – let me know what you do.

Yours in sympathy
Jackie

From: sara@e-mail.com

To: jackie@e-mail.com

Sent: 31 July

Subject: The moaners

Dear Jackie

Thanks for your help earlier today. I took the option of asking the participants what they wanted to do. Interestingly, the majority wanted to complete the programme as planned as they felt some of the issues where not relevant to all of them. I got an interesting reaction from the two who were moaning, though! One said that he was surprised that I thought this had been happening, as he hadn't noticed it! When I told him that he'd said a few things this morning that had made me think there was a problem, he was in total shock. He hadn't realized he was doing it. Consequently, he went on to be very good in the afternoon, and joined in fully. The other person said that she did have some issues and she wondered why her manager wasn't attending this programme! I agreed with her that as the others didn't want to spend any more time on this, we would meet tomorrow and talk through her concerns.

The rest of my day was good and we managed to finish the course on time and with a positive feeling.

Thanks again.

Sara

From:	sara@e-mail.com
To:	jackie@e-mail.com
Sent:	4 August
Subject:	How much should we pass on to line managers?

Dear Jackie

In your e-mail last week advising me what to do with my 'moaners', you suggested I should tell the participants' line manager about the problems I'd had.

I'm a bit concerned about the whole area of what kinds of things should be reported further, especially as at the start of every course I agree a ground rule of 'confidentiality'. Where does this start and finish? I've always worked on the basis that what happens in the training room stays in the training room, but then, until I got this job, I wasn't really an in-company trainer. How do you know what to share and what to keep to yourself?

Regards
Sara

From: jackie@e-mail.com

To: sara@e-mail.com

Sent: 4 August

Subject: Confidentiality

Dear Sara

This is a difficult, ethical question as you have responsibilities both to the line managers and to your participants. I use the following guidelines to help me decide what and how to pass information on:

- I never give names – who said what is not as important as what was said and why.
- If it is obvious who said what, for example because a line manager only has one member on a course, I give feedback to all the managers together.
- I talk about issues raised on the course in general terms. I try to use statements like 'During the course discussions, several trainees said they were concerned about staff motivation' or 'Having just trained this course, I think there might be an issue with the cascade of information in some of the teams; is this something you've noticed?'.
- If there is something I think is a specific problem for someone, I encourage them to talk to their line manager or suggest that we do it together, with me as the facilitator or independent person.
- When I've learnt about someone's specific problem, I try to think of different ways of addressing the issue. I might include it as a case study on a management course, or bring it up as an example at a general management meeting, where the relevant line manager might be present.

Sometimes I must admit I'm quite passive and simply drop hints to the line manager like 'Some of the other departments have a problem with cascading information, how do you do it?' or 'I was talking to some staff from the other building and they were saying that their manager does such and such'. I don't know if it works or whether in our 'assertive world' we should do it, but I feel better afterwards.

Regards
Jackie

From:	sara@e-mail.com
To:	jackie@e-mail.com
Sent:	9 May
Subject:	Can you do this training in two hours rather than a day?

Jackie

Why do line managers always think we can train everything in just a couple of hours? I've just had yet another telephone call from a line manager asking why a course is listed as taking four days – he said, and I quote, 'I could show them that in a matter of hours'.

I find it so frustrating that managers want everything to happen in the least amount of time, and yet when things go wrong or people can't do what they are supposed to, they always blame training!

What do you do to get over this? Today, I explained to the line manager that whilst the theory could be covered quite quickly, it was important to give trainees the opportunity to try out the underlying skills and also to check that the information was properly understood. I said that what really takes the time is ensuring that the knowledge and skills are fully learnt, and that they're not forgotten the moment the person steps back into his or her office.

I'm welcome your thoughts on how to get line managers to understand more about what we do.

Sara

From: jackie@e-mail.com

To: sara@e-mail.com

Sent: 9 May

Subject: Can you do this training in two hours rather than a day?

Dear Sara

I think you already have the answer to this issue. As you said in your e-mail, all we can do is explain about how adults learn and how important it is that trainees get an opportunity to prove their knowledge or practise their new skills in a safe environment.

You could help this conversation by referring back to the learning objectives. Like me, I know you use the technique of listing what the trainees will be able to do at the end of the course/event. So from this you can identify what they will not be able to achieve by the end of the course, or how you will have to change the objectives because you have less time. For example:

- Old objectives. After the course participants will be able to:
  - use various communication techniques;
  - implement strategies for dealing with customers;
  - behave more assertively when handling customers.

- New objectives. After the course participants will be able to:
  - identify various communication techniques;
  - list different strategies about how to handle customers;
  - describe what assertive behaviour is.

As you can see, the new objectives don't describe participants actually doing anything other than listing facts – this means that they've learnt the theory but doesn't necessary mean that they'll be able to implement it in practice.

I suppose once you have made it clear what you can and can not achieve in the time allocated it's up to the manager to decide if he is willing to live with it. Something I always do now, especially in these cases, is get the manager to sign off on the aims, objectives and content, so that he or she can't complain later. Well actually managers can complain and do, but I can prove that I delivered what they asked for!

Jackie

From: sara@e-mail.com

To: jackie@e-mail.com

Sent: 2 June

Subject: Music is the spice of life

Dear Jackie

I went on a great course yesterday about accelerated learning techniques. I was really impressed by what they said about how to use music to enhance learning. Apparently if you use the right music (baroque, for example) you can help people learn more effectively.

I'm going to try it and see if it works. I'll let you know how I get on!

Regards
Sara

From: sara@e-mail.com

To: jackie@e-mail.com

Sent: 2 September

Subject: Music is the spice of life

Dear Jackie

I've been playing around with music during different courses, and thought you might like to share the experience!

The first time I tried it, I played a pop music tape at the start of the course and during a long group activity. It didn't really work the way I thought it would! During the group activity, several people sang along with the lyrics, and at times seemed to be listening and singing more than they were working! I think my choice of music was wrong!

Since then, I have tried playing some upbeat music before courses actually start. This seems to go down quite well and it's given the trainees something to talk about when they're nervous or don't really know each other.

I've also been playing baroque music during practice time on system courses – normally everyone is concentrating so hard on using the system, the room is really quiet. Putting the music on quietly in the background has made the atmosphere better and seems to help them work faster – you can almost hear the keyboards going in time to the music!

I'm still experimenting with different tunes, but so far, I think I'm a convert!

Sara

From:	jackie@e-mail.com
To:	sara@e-mail.com
Sent:	27 January
Subject:	A trainee who refuses to join in

Dear Sara

I'm in the middle of a two-day course and I have a problem! One of the participants has refused to join in one of the group activities. She started by saying that she didn't want to do the activity and that she would watch from the sidelines.

I said that I wanted her to participate and that the others would not be very impressed if she didn't. She wouldn't tell me why she didn't want to join in, and said that she was an adult and if she chose not to do something, no one could make her!

Consequently, she didn't join in and she spent the afternoon just watching the others, so she didn't have anything to contribute to the post-activity discussion either! I feel that we're in conflict – you know, that feeling when you're sure someone is annoyed or upset with you. I have to say I'm very annoyed with her – what is the point of coming on the course and not taking part?

The second day of the course is tomorrow and if she turns up I'm not sure what to do or say. Any ideas on how I can handle her? I would also be interested to know how you would have dealt with her today.

Thanks.

Jackie

From: sara@e-mail.com

To: jackie@e-mail.com

Sent: 27 November

Subject: A trainee who refuses to join in

Dear Jackie

I wonder what her problem is? Is it the type of activity or something else? I had someone like this some years ago when I was training values and attitudes. In my case, it was that the person was scared of the subject matter and wanted the security of seeing what happened before she committed herself. I didn't realize this until afterwards, when she said that she wished she'd joined in, as everyone else seemed to have fun. The subject was heavy, and we'd agreed that whilst full participation was required, if at any time someone wanted to take personal time out they could.

Getting annoyed with your trainee won't help, all it'll do is stop you dealing with the real problem. The difficulty with us (humans, that is) is that when we start getting emotional, we often stop being objective, and start reacting. We then either start communicating in either 'child' or 'parent' mode (transactional analysis theory), and behaviour breeds behaviour, so the other person responds accordingly. From reading your e-mail it seems that by telling her that you wanted her to participate and 'that the others would not be very impressed if she didn't', you were in 'critical parent'. She behaved in a 'child' way – I don't want to, I won't tell you why!

The 'adult' way, which is to use logical problem-solving and compromise, would be more guaranteed to gain a win–win position, and avoid the conflict you described. The 'adult' response to her refusal to join in might have been to say, 'I would like you to join in, however, if you prefer not to, perhaps you could watch the activity and give the others feedback based on your observations'. After all, did it really matter if she did or did not do the activity? Or were you upset because she didn't do what you wanted her to do?

The whole issue about taking part is difficult. I do understand what you are saying when you ask what's the point if they are not going to participate, but then, if they are still learning by watching others, perhaps we need to ...

Cont.

... support that. The danger is that by making them to something that they don't want to do, or believe they can't do, they won't learn anyway.

I don't think you'll like this, but I suppose I'm saying 'Chill out' and don't make any more of an issue about it. When she turns up tomorrow, don't refer to it unless she does.

Hope you're not annoyed with me now! Let me know how it goes.

Sara

From:	jackie@e-mail.com
To:	sara@e-mail.com
Sent:	28 January
Subject:	A trainee who refuses to join in

Dear Sara

Much as I hate to admit it, you're probably right, I was reacting to the fact that she didn't want to join in my session. I suppose, if I'm honest, I took it personally!

Well, today she didn't turn up, so I didn't have to deal with her. However, her manager phoned my boss and said that she was upset because of my authoritarian approach. First thing tomorrow, I have to explain myself!

Oh dear! I hope I can explain the situation.

Jackie

From:	jackie@e-mail.com
To:	sara@e-mail.com
Sent:	28 January
Subject:	A trainee who refuses to join in

Dear Sara

The saga continues. I met with my line manager this morning and explained what had happened and why I thought it had got out of hand. I was very calm and made sure that I accepted ownership of my behaviour. I told him that I had learnt a lot from the experience and that now I would handle it differently. He was really very supportive and recommended that I see the trainee and 'repair' the relationship. So, we've just had lunch together.

The short version is that I apologized for being aggressive and explained why I'd reacted the way I had. She apologized for her behaviour and explained that she hadn't wanted to do the activity because she'd just found out she's pregnant and she was feeling sick. She hadn't wanted to explain in front of everyone else as she didn't want everyone knowing about the baby yet. She'd felt pushed into a corner by my reaction.

Well, it just goes to show that you need to understand what's happening to the other person before you can make judgements. We got on really well, and I have promised to keep her secret.

Thank you for making me reflect on my own motives and behaviour.

Jackie

From: jackie@e-mail.com

To: sara@e-mail.com

Sent: 9 April

Subject: Self-study packages

Sara

I'm in the process of setting up a self-study library. This follows a survey that we did with our staff asking them about their interests and their willingness to study in this way. The response was very good and it seems that people are really keen to learn.

I've got several questions:

- How can I maintain the momentum once the library has been up and running for a few months?
- How do I monitor the use of the materials?
- What should I be doing in order to back up the learning through the self-study packs?
- How can I make sure the materials are constantly updated without costing us a fortune?
- How can I monitor the return on investment?

I know you've used self-study in the past and I was wondering if you have any thoughts.

Look forward to hearing from you.

Jackie

From:	sara@e-mail.com
To:	jackie@e-mail.com
Sent:	9 April
Subject:	Self-study packages

Dear Jackie

Yes, I've played with the idea of self-study packages, with various degrees of success. At my last company we had a self-development area, which anyone could come along and use. The videos and computer-based training (CBT) packages were on shelves and people would book the room through our secretary. We didn't, therefore, have much of a system for identifying who used what, or for really following up on learning. As I think I said, my role was more recruitment than training, so although I was interested in doing more with the concept, I never had the time!

Here, we have a library of books and packages, which people can borrow. That way, we know who's got what and can follow up on how they got on with it. We encourage people to use it in the personnel and training office so that we can help if they need assistance. Staff don't tend to use the material that much – they seem to prefer to go on courses. I probably use some of the packages more to help me design or deliver courses!

I've just started to proactively encourage use of the library as an alternative to courses. We've sent the list of resources out to all staff, and I've written a brief article for the in-house magazine about how useful these resources can be. The last time I got asked for a report-writing course, I told the person to use our self-study pack rather than go on a course.

I'm also interested in getting some of the CBT packages on to our network so that people can use them at their desks. I think this might encourage the staff to use them more – it'll be like playing a game rather than working. This involves having licences that allow you to put them on more than one PC, and these can be expensive.

So as you can see, I have some experience of self-study but am by no means an expert.

Sara

From:	jackie@e-mail.com
To:	sara@e-mail.com
Sent:	29 May
Subject:	Self-study packages

Dear Sara

I've decided to start small on the self-study approach, partly because of your experience and partly because I saw how much some of these materials cost! So, from our survey, we picked 10 topics that people said that they would be interested in, and have bought either a CBT or self-study pack. We set aside a corner of the office and made it the Self-Development Desk. Then we did the following marketing:

- A flyer to all staff telling them what we had bought, and explaining why self-study and CBT is such a good idea.
- A competition asking 15 questions about the self-development area and the packages – some involved using the CBTs, others were about who is in which video or how long is the cassette in this pack. The prize was either a meal for two or a book or record token of the same value. Of 400 staff, 150 entered the competition!
- An invitation to certain people to come and use the CBTs and study packs – we contacted the people who'd asked on the original survey for materials on the 10 topics we'd picked.

We've had a lot of interest, but it is still the first month! I've asked for people to book to use the area, so I can monitor what's being used and by whom. I'm hoping I'll be able to evaluate the learning by sending out one of our standard post-course evaluation forms. I've worked out that to get a good return on the investment, I have to get 100 people to use the area in the first year.

Here's hoping.

Jackie

From: sara@e-mail.com

To: jackie@e-mail.com

Sent: 29 May

Subject: Self-study packages

Dear Jackie

Thanks for your update about your self-study area. We've put two packages on to our network, but we've found that people haven't been using them. It seems that when they are at their own desks, they think they should be working!

The good news is that one of our managers is such a convert to training and development that he's set aside a desk in his department solely for staff to use these packages, or others they've borrowed from me. This seems to be working much better than getting people to do this at their own desks – and I think they want him to see them using the packages.

Talk soon.

Sara

From:	jackie@e-mail.com
To:	sara@e-mail.com
Sent:	8 May
Subject:	Induction

Sara

Did you tell me that you've just written a new corporate induction package? I've been asked to put together a package which will include one day in the training room and then some ongoing self-study.

I want to make sure that delegates really get something from this training – ie that they're introduced to the company and its culture, that they meet the people they need to meet, that they are introduced to the fundamentals of their job roles and that they know where they need to go for things like stationery and computer support.

What do you think?

I would like some ideas on activities and structure please.

Thanks.

Jackie

From: sara@e-mail.com

To: jackie@e-mail.com

Sent: 9 May

Subject: Induction

Dear Jackie

Induction is probably the one thing that I hate training the most! I don't really know why, but it just doesn't challenge me at all!

This is why I've just changed the course here. I used to train the whole day, with the exception of the Health and Safety section, which the H&S officer used to come in and do. We have quite a large turnover of staff, and were doing induction twice a month! The course was quite static and depended on a lot of input from me. It's really difficult to make an organization chart sound interesting!

I did a little research about different styles of inducting staff, and asked a few people how it worked in their organizations. There seemed to be four approaches:

- Running a one-day course where different key people from the organization came and talked about their areas.
- Leaving line managers to induct new staff themselves, sometimes with a checklist to follow.
- Providing a booklet explaining about the company, or, in one case, a video.
- Setting learning objectives that the new member of staff has to achieve in a given period – this method is used by the local police service.

Some books and people suggested a combination of these.

I'm not sure there is one right answer – I think this depends on the culture of your company and the level of the people joining. We've gone for a combination of a half-day course, with myself, the H&S officer and one of the directors as a guest speaker, and the checklist for line managers. I've also made the methods more fun and participative, which means I feel better about delivering it!

Sara

From: jackie@e-mail.com

To: sara@e-mail.com

Sent: 29 June

Subject: Induction

Dear Sara

I thought I'd update you on what I decided to do about the induction course. Thanks for the ideas, by the way.

I've gone for a combination approach. We're using a full-day course, where a representative from each department comes to explain what their department does and how it fits into the company. We also cover Health and Safety, where different things are and quality assurance. The MD has agreed to come and do a 'welcome to the company' opening session! We also give all new staff a development booklet, which has about 15 learning objectives in it. They have to achieve the objectives by attending the course, and also with the help of their line manager/supervisor – line managers are responsible for ensuring that they achieve them within the first two weeks of joining the company.

We're also trying to recruit to the course dates, so that new staff are not in the company for some weeks before they get their induction course.

We've only done one to date, but it seemed better!

Jackie

From:	sara@e-mail.com
To:	jackie@e-mail.com
Sent:	3 June
Subject:	Outdoor training

Dear Jackie

Have you got any experience of outdoor training? I met with a company last week that specializes in this type of training, and personally was very interested. As you know, I do a fair amount of hillwalking, and have in the past done some canoeing, camping and rock climbing. I'm wondering whether to put forward this company as a potential provider of our team-building courses. But I want to make sure that I'm not just doing so because I fancy a week or two in the open!

What do you know about these courses?

Sara

From:	jackie@e-mail.com
To:	sara@e-mail.com
Sent:	6 June
Subject:	Outdoor training

Dear Sara

I think you know how much I dislike being outdoors, so whenever I could I've avoided outdoor training! Having said this, I do have some thoughts that might help you in your deliberations.

Think about the training cycle and go back to your objectives. What do you want to gain from the training? What do you want people to do as a result of the training? Then consider whether outdoor training is the best way of achieving your objectives.

Consider how you expect the delegates to implement their learning. I have found that generally people do enjoy getting away from the real world for a while and that some really strong bonds can develop between individuals who have been away together.

In some ways this is a good thing, however, if a team member hasn't been able to be part of the group for some reason, they can become really alienated from the team. So think about whether you'll be able to send whole teams away together. In my experience this really is the only way to run these things. If you send people from different teams away together, they tend to find that they have a good time, they meet people from elsewhere in the company, but they have huge trouble in implementing any action plans they've made.

Consider the equal opportunities issues. Will everybody be able to spend time away from home? Do you have any individuals with disabilities and will the training provider be able to meet their needs? Do you have anybody (like me) who is fairly phobic about heights and confined spaces – what will be provided for these people or will they be forced into situations that they are not ready to deal with? Do you have any individuals with health issues such as heart problems or back problems and how will their specific needs be met? ...

... Ask questions about the training provider. What qualifications do they have? Are they registered with the relevant bodies, eg BCU (British Canoeing Union) and do they work to those bodies' standards? What is their experience of working with groups? What challenges have they faced and how have they dealt with them? What arrangements do they make for dealing with emergencies? Are the instructors all trained in First Aid? How do they maintain their equipment in good working order? I would also suggest that you need to visit the venues they'll be using and do a thorough inspection of the facilities – if you have a Safety specialist available, take him or her with you.

My overall advice is to really think about why you're doing this kind of training. I feel very strongly that you could spend huge sums of money implementing this programme and then not see any tangible results at the end of it, other than the fact that people have had a good time. If this is the real objective, then that's fine. If you want business benefits then you need to be absolutely certain that you have firm strategies in place for follow-up after the course. This means that you must have all the managers on your side, since it'll be their job to ensure that action plans are actually put into action.

As a final note, I must tell you that I *did* actually go on an outdoor course and I quite enjoyed it – well, it wasn't as bad as I was expecting. However, there was no follow-up after the course, my action plan stayed in my folder and the whole thing is now a distant memory. DON'T let this happen to your people.

Hope this helps.

Jackie

From: sara@e-mail.com

To: jackie@e-mail.com

Sent: 12 June

Subject: Outdoor training

Dear Jackie

Thanks for your e-mail about outdoor training. Your comments have made me think even more about why I wanted to do the training. I'm working with line managers at the moment on their role in staff development, and I've decided to put the outdoor training on hold until this is completed.

This will give me time to investigate the training provider more thoroughly and to consider how I'll ensure that we do get a return on our investment in outdoor training. I do believe people should enjoy training, but I need to make sure that they get more out of it than just having a good time!

I'll let you know how I get on.

Have a good long weekend in Paris. I'll speak to you when you get back.

Sara

From:	sara@e-mail.com
To:	jackie@e-mail.com
Sent:	25 September
Subject:	Outdoor training

Dear Jackie

Just wanted to let you know that I have just been a participant on some team-building training. The training involved some outdoor activities and I think it worked really well.

The course was not one of these that involved rock climbing or canoeing, basically it involved a combination of work that took place indoors and outdoors. The training took place at a beautiful old country house, with lovely grounds and acres of space. We spent our mornings mainly in the training room and then after lunch we did various outdoor activities, eg building structures from poles and rope, and taking part in trust games and parachute games. These activities were effective for a number of reasons:

They got us outside and moving around at a time when we may have been dozing off after a huge lunch!

Everyone could be involved in some way; there was no requirement for stamina or strength.

The trainer made sure that at the end of every activity there was a through debriefing about the activity, why the activity was included and how the learning points related to our lives at work.

Each of us made an action plan and the trainer will be coming to visit us at work to have a meeting with each individual and their line manager in order to discuss how we will be implementing the action plan at work.

Thank you for your comments! I think they saved us time and money!

Sara

From: jackie@e-mail.com

To: sara@e-mail.com

Sent: 31 March

Subject: Giving the bad news

Dear Sara

I'm currently running a series of new starter courses for one of our departments. It's quite exciting really: because of new business this department needs to recruit and train another 25 people, who will start work by the end of April. I think the department staff and I are working really well together – not only have we agreed the content, aims and objectives of the course, we've also worked on clear performance criteria.

The criteria consist of the productivity and quality figures that staff in the department are expected to achieve at the end of the course, after their first month, and then after three months (by which time they will be at the same level as the experienced 'older' staff). I was really pleased with this as it meant we had a really clear measurement to train to, and the trainees will know what's expected of them in the first few months.

Great – until I got someone who is not at the required standard. The department head wants me to tell this delegate that unfortunately he's failed the course and lost his job. How do I do that? It seems to be against everything that we work to achieve; I've always approached training with the view that so long as someone is developing, however small the progress, then we're achieving our goals.

Help – I need some ideas on how to tell this person and what to do if he says it's my fault because the training wasn't good enough.

Jackie

From:	sara@e-mail.com
To:	jackie@e-mail.com
Sent:	3 April
Subject:	Giving the bad news

Jackie

You really do come up with some goodies don't you!

I do sympathize with you on this one – I think you hit the nail on the head in your final sentence: 'What do I do if this person says it's my fault because the training wasn't good enough?'. I think the reason we don't like giving people the bad news is because we feel it reflects on us. Well I suppose that in some senses it does, however you're not saying that you couldn't train the person if you had more time available or if there were more resources. The real issue here is that you have a certain budget of time and money and that if a person doesn't achieve the required standards within that budget then you're required to move on to the next person. This may not seem fair at the moment, but it is a hard economic fact – and you are working in a business setting.

So how do you go about giving the news to the delegate?

Firstly, at the start of a programme that has a pass or fail you must ensure that all the delegates are aware of the standards expected of them plus the implications of not achieving those standards. Now I know that you're a trained assessor and so I'm sure you did this at the beginning of the process.

Secondly, you should be building in regular interim assessments so that the individuals can be supported if they're not meeting the required standards during the training; 'formative assessment' is its 'proper' name. If this part of the process is effective then the individual who isn't achieving the standards won't be surprised when they come to the final, summative, assessment.

Thirdly, you need to use all your skills in giving feedback in a constructive and supportive manner. You must ensure that the person doesn't feel like a failure. They simply haven't achieved the required standard within the ...

Cont.

... constraints that exist. It would also be very positive if you were able to suggest other options for the individual in other areas of work, within or outside the company.

Finally, your delegate may turn round to you and tell you that he's failed because your training was not up to scratch. You should be able to counter this by knowing that you have good evaluation processes in place. I'm sure that you regularly review the effectiveness of your training, by self-evaluation and reflection and using peer and line manager reviews.

I think that you'll have all the processes in place, if you're working in the way you always used to, so now it's time to put on your brave face and do the dirty deed!

Good luck – call me if you want to talk about it.

Sara.

From:	jackie@e-mail.com
To:	sara@e-mail.com
Sent:	3 April
Subject:	Giving the bad news

Sara

Thanks for your e-mail. You were right, I did have all the processes in place, what I needed was some reassurance and a bit of a prod in the right direction. I was obviously in a really wimpy mood!

When I spoke to the delegate he wasn't at all surprised by what I said. In fact he told me it was a relief since from early in the training course he knew that he wouldn't enjoy doing the job anyway!

All that worry over nothing.

Thanks for your help.

Jackie

From: jackie@e-mail.com

To: sara@e-mail.com

Sent: 5 May

Subject: Technophobe

Dear Sara

I had someone on a Word course today who seems to be a real technophobe. He'd been sent on the course because he doesn't really use the PC on his desk, and his manager wants him to try and use the secretaries less. He just seemed to be really scared of pressing the buttons and what the system might do if he did. He even joked that he preferred the old-fashioned methods of pen and paper.

We are just having a break, so if you get this e-mail, please come back with any ideas you might have as soon as possible.

Look forward to hearing from you.

Jackie

E-mail 95

From:	sara@e-mail.com
To:	jackie@e-mail.com
Sent:	5 May
Subject:	Technophobe

Jackie

Got your e-mail and hope that this gets to you in time to be of some assistance.

I think this is one of those situations where you need to persevere with the person for the rest of the day and then suggest that he come back for some one-to-one coaching.

Many people who haven't been faced with a computer before are worried about what will happen if they press the wrong buttons. I think the thing to do is tell your delegate that it'll be very difficult for him to break anything. Even if he does hit the wrong key this won't be a problem and sometimes what seems a big problem can be sorted out just by turning the machine off and on again.

I'm sure you'll handle the situation tactfully, just make sure that you don't undermine his confidence by pointing out to other members of the group that he is struggling.

When you get him on a one-to-one basis, go through details like the basics of how the computer works, the function of each part and what the different screen icons mean. To get him used to using the mouse, you may want to have him playing some of the games that are usually on PCs, like Solitaire.

When you get into the actual Word package, go through with him the very simplest functions. Make sure that he has time to practise as you're going through each bit and try to give him some fun activities to do.

This whole issue is about confidence. You must use all your patience and your empathy – imagine what you would be like if someone were trying to get you to go rock climbing! ...

Cont.

... So, here are the main suggestions for you try:

- Support him for the rest of the day. This includes reassuring him that he can't break the computer.
- Get him back for a one-to-one session.
- Go back to basics, showing him that the computer really doesn't bite.
- Be patient with him.
- Empathize with him.
- Give him fun activities to do.
- Don't be afraid to take one step back for every step forward.

If you get a chance now, before the others come back, maybe you could do some of this reassurance and support, if not then as soon as possible.

All the best
Sara.

From:	jackie@e-mail.com
To:	sara@e-mail.com
Sent:	6 May
Subject:	Technophobe

Sara

Thanks for getting back to me yesterday. The situation with my technophobe seems to be resolved.

After I'd read your e-mail I went back to the training room and luckily my delegate was there on his own. We started to talk about how the course was going and he really opened up about how much his job has changed and how he's really uncomfortable with computers. He was saying that he's tried to use his son's machine at home, but feels really silly every time his seven-year-old can do things quicker than he can.

He asked me if I thought he should leave the course as he felt that he was holding everyone else back. I said that it would be his decision, that I could give him some exercises and games to be practising on or that he could leave it for today and come back for a one-to-one training session. In the end he decided to go and I told the group that he had been called away on a personal matter. I'm seeing him this afternoon for his first training session and I'll make sure we go back to basics, but in a sensitive and constructive way.

Thanks for your help on this one.

Jackie

From:	sara@e-mail.com
To:	jackie@e-mail.com
Sent:	30 May
Subject:	Technophobe

Jackie

Interesting that we should have been discussing computer training. I had an experience this week that has really highlighted the need for prerequisite skills on this type of training.

We were training a group of temporary staff to use our in-house computer system. We only had two days to train them and so it was really important to focus on the job that they would be doing. One of the delegates during the introductions at the start mentioned that she had never used a computer before. This was painfully obvious as we started the actual session – she didn't know how to use the mouse and was getting completely lost. I had to take her aside at the morning break and explain to her that we wouldn't be able to train her in the time available and therefore she wouldn't be able to complete the course.

I've spoken to our personnel team and explained to them exactly how we work and what requirements there are for our temporary staff. I'd wrongly assumed they knew!

Sara

From: sara@e-mail.com

To: jackie@e-mail.com

Sent: 1 November

Subject: Touch a raw nerve!

Dear Jackie

I think I've really done it today! Towards the end of the afternoon, we were doing a role-play about a poor performer. I was playing the part of the poor performer and one of the participants took the part of the manager. The others were watching, so that they could give feedback to the 'manager' about how he handled the situation.

When he started to tell me that I was going to be disciplined because my work was so bad, I told him (in role) that actually I had problems at home as my partner was terminally ill. He handled it well and asked me to tell him about it – which I did.

At this point, one of the trainees ran out of the room. Well, I couldn't follow because I was in the middle of the exercise. One of the other participants went out. By the time we'd finished, I called a break and went to find them. I found the second one, who said that Joanne was upset because the role-play was very like her home situation. It was almost the end of the day, and Joanne had gone home, so I didn't get chance to speak to her at all. Now I feel very guilty – both about being insensitive and not speaking to her before she went home tonight!

Should I talk to her in the morning about this?

Sara

From: jackie@e-mail.com

To: sara@e-mail.com

Sent: 1 November

Subject: Touch a raw nerve!

Sara

First of all I would say *don't* feel guilty. We can't possibly know everything that's going on in our delegates' lives and if we did, we'd probably never get any training done at all.

I think it will be helpful for both of you if you follow up with the person tomorrow – it'll help appease the feelings you're having, and show her that you did notice what was going on.

I suggest you telephone the delegate tomorrow and tell her that you were sorry to have missed her yesterday afternoon. Ask her if you can see her for a coffee to discuss what she missed at the end of the session and to give her the opportunity to discuss any issues that she'd like to raise. Make it clear to her that you won't ask her to discuss anything that she doesn't feel comfortable with.

If she says 'No' to your invitation, then don't allow this to make you feel even guiltier than you do already. Say to her that you're aware something upset her yesterday and you're sorry about this. If she does want to talk to you let her know that you're available.

If she says 'Yes' to your invitation, then when you meet with her reiterate that she doesn't have to discuss anything she feels uncomfortable with, but say that you're aware something upset her yesterday and would like to offer your support. From here the conversation may or may not develop. I know you have excellent listening skills and I can only suggest that at this point you use them! If you have the opportunity, explain to her that you had no idea that your role-play would be so close to any real-life situations and that, had you known, you would have given her the opportunity to leave the room or you would have changed the scenario.

One final word of comfort; I think that when you are having real problems outside work, any little thing can set you off. I believe that your delegate did ...

... the right thing by leaving the room and so long as you let her know that the situation was unfortunate but unintentional everything will be resolved. I also feel that if you don't approach the delegate tomorrow, you'll be constantly worried about bumping into her, or about the next time you see her in a session.

I'll be thinking of you tomorrow morning.

All the very best with this one.

Jackie

From: sara@e-mail.com

To: jackie@e-mail.com

Sent: 2 November

Subject: Touch a raw nerve!

Jackie

Thanks for your comments about my situation with the role-playing and the delegate who left the room.

I did what you suggested and gave her a call to invite her for a coffee. She turned me down flat! I told her that I was sorry if the situation in the role-play had been upsetting for her and explained that I had never meant to cause anyone in the group distress. I also said that, should she wish to meet to discuss the course any further, she should not hesitate to contact me. I have to say that she was very offhand with me and I'm still battling with some guilty feelings. I guess these will pass with time. At least I don't feel worried about seeing her around the offices now.

I was discussing this situation with our personnel manager today and she has offered to be available for the next course that I run on this topic so that, should someone get upset, she could support them whilst I continue with the role-play.

The other thing I'm considering doing is bringing in some professional actors to do the role-playing; this will allow me to support the group and to facilitate the discussions about the role-play.

Thanks for getting back to me so quickly on this one.

Sara

From:	jackie@e-mail.com
To:	sara@e-mail.com
Sent:	28 February
Subject:	The back-turner

Dear Sara

I had a really strange person in my group today. Every time we spoke to him and he didn't agree with us, he turned his back on us. It was usually me, but on four occasions I noticed he did it to other participants.

Any ideas on how I could handle this?

Jackie

From: sara@e-mail.com

To: jackie@e-mail.com

Sent: 28 February

Subject: The back-turner

Jackie

Just got your e-mail and thought that I would respond straight away. It sounds like your delegate has some real issues with being able to listen to other people's viewpoints. I have a couple of suggestions for you:

- Ignore his behaviour and simply continue with the session regardless – he will probably turn back to the group eventually.
- Steer the discussion around to talking about body language (this may be appropriate, it depends on your topic) and ask the group what different types of body language say to the rest of the group – this might make him think about the message he is sending.
- Ask a question and then ask him for his specific thoughts – he would, I imagine, turn back to discuss the issue. If he doesn't, you'll be able to ask him if there is a problem.
- Take him aside during one of the breaks and ask him if there is a specific problem, since he appears not to want to discuss some issues.
- Reiterate the ground rule, if you are using it, about listening willingly and attentively to the viewpoints of others.

Don't let this person get to you – as long as his behaviour is not affecting the group and you attempt to address it, I think that will be fine.

Sara

From:	sara@e-mail.com
To:	jackie@e-mail.com
Sent:	31 October
Subject:	Residential courses

Jackie

I don't know if you've got any ideas on this one: I'm running a three-day residential programme for new managers. During the day we'll be doing a variety of activities ranging from quizzes to team-building to input on management theory. The MD has asked me to arrange the evening entertainment for both evenings and I'm stumped. All the activities that I can think of are very much about learning and I think that by the evenings delegates will be worn out. I want to do something that will be (a) fun (b) appealing to all the delegates (they range in age from 24 to 49) and (c) easy to co-ordinate.

Do you have any experience of this sort of thing? I am starting to feel a bit like a Redcoat at Butlin's!

Yours hopefully
Sara

E-mail 104

From: jackie@e-mail.com

To: sara@e-mail.com

Sent: 5 November

Subject: Residential courses

Sara

I have to say that I don't like this question very much. I've been wracking my brains over things that I may have done or seen in the past and I've come up with the following ideas:

- An auction – either using real money or 'Monopoly' money! I remember doing an activity based on an auction. We worked in teams with a set amount of money we could spend on a list of items. As a team we had to come to a consensus about what we wanted to bid for and how high we would go for each item. The team that got the most for their money was the winner and got a prize – a bottle of wine I seem to recall.
- A talent show. Ask each delegate to compete in a show. They can sing, tell jokes or whatever! I have to say that some people will not be keen on this one, but if you really want to be a Redcoat…
- A pub quiz. You can organize teams for this and use questions from a quiz book or one of the board games that is based on general knowledge questions. You could even have a round based on the topic of the training or on company knowledge. Most people do enjoy quizzes, so this one would involve everyone.
- A scavenger hunt. Put delegates into teams and give them a list of items they must find within a set amount of time. The list could include obscure things like a postcard of the Eiffel Tower, a chef's hat and so on.
- 'Pictionary'. If you don't know, this is a board game which a drawing version of charades. You play in teams and it really is good fun.

I suggest you choose one activity for each night on the course. I think delegates will appreciate some time simply to socialize, but by organizing one activity for each night you will have fulfilled your MD's request.

Hope it all goes well.

Jackie

From:	jackie@e-mail.com
To:	sara@e-mail.com
Sent:	17 July
Subject:	Videos

Sara

After a couple of my recent courses delegates have written on their evaluation forms that they'd like to have seen some videos on the topics covered.

In the past when I've used videos I've found that they're sometimes the only thing that people remember and they don't necessarily reinforce the learning points that I wanted to get across.

I'm wondering if you have any tips on how to select a video. All the brochures that I have look incredibly appealing, but the tapes are so expensive, even to hire, that I want to make sure I get value for money.

Help me please!

Jackie

From:	sara@e-mail.com
To:	jackie@e-mail.com
Sent:	20 July
Subject:	Videos

Jackie

I know what you mean about all the videos sounding good, but being very expensive.

I picked up on your comment about the video being the only thing that the delegates remember. I'm not sure this is necessarily such a bad thing, at least they've remembered something and we can hope they'll have learnt from relating the video to their own experience.

I think that so many people are used to watching TV and using computers, if they don't have something like a video to watch, they feel hard-done-by.

I recommend that you ask the video providers if they have a previewing centre. This is a really good way to view a whole set of videos without needing to pay for the preview tapes. I've spent a whole day before now, in London, visiting various video providers and watching videos. This is harder work than it sounds and I recommend that you make notes because if you don't you'll forget which video was which!

I think the questions to ask yourself are the same questions that you ask for any training method that you are selecting, ie 'How will using this video help me to achieve my objectives?'; 'Does this video reinforce my messages?'; 'How will watching this video help delegates to learn?'.

I would suggest that you watch any video that you choose a number of times before using it so that you're completely familiar with every learning point and can discuss it with the group. I also suggest that you consider using the video in small chunks rather than as a whole. This means you integrate it more into the whole training and it's not seen as a stand-alone 'thing'.

I've used a video most successfully when I've prepared delegates to watch it by asking them to complete a questionnaire containing questions relevant to the video and the training objectives. After watching the video I've asked ...

... delegates to complete and discuss another questionnaire. This way delegates discuss how the video is relevant to the 'real world' and how they might apply its learning points.

If you do buy or hire any packages you'll find that they usually come with materials for the trainer to use and ideas on how to incorporate the video into a training session. All I would say is, use the video as only one of a variety of learning methods that you choose. Make sure you have plenty of activities and time for reflection to meet the learning styles of your delegates.

By the way if you get any packages, I'd be really interested to have a look at what you have bought!

Speak to you soon.

Sara

From: sara@e-mail.com

To: jackie@e-mail.com

Sent: 17 August

Subject: Action planning

Jackie

I'm thinking about the programmes I'll be running in the autumn and I'm a bit concerned about the action plans I've been using in the past. I'm very aware that delegates go away from the courses all fired up and full of great plans, but very often the plans are pushed to one side once they get back to their desks.

What can you tell me about how you use action plans? What successes have you had? What problems have you faced? What are you thinking about trying?

Look forward to hearing from you.

Sara

From:	jackie@e-mail.com
To:	sara@e-mail.com
Sent:	31 August
Subject:	Action planning

Sara

Sorry that it has taken me a while to get back to you – I've been away for a brief holiday. I am feeling refreshed and revived and almost raring to go now!

So – action plans, eh? Well, I think that I must have been experiencing much the same problems as you, in that my delegates all complete action plans, but the plans very rarely come to fruition.

I'm going to try a new approach this time. I'm going to issue the action plans before the course – I'll ask the delegates to complete their plans with their line manager as part of the course nomination process. I'm not going to accept any nominations without action plans attached. This may seem a little harsh but I think that it'll ensure that managers are supporting their staff throughout the learning process.

On the action plans (which I'm calling 'Learning Plans') I'm going to ask the following questions:

- What is your current job role?
- What are the main objectives for your role for the next six months?
- What are your personal (work-related) objectives for the next six months?
- What do you need to learn in order to fulfil the objectives of your role and your personal objectives?
- How will the programme that you are applying for help you to meet your learning needs?
- What support will you need from your line manager and your team in order to meet your learning needs?
- How will you and your line manager know when your learning needs have been fulfilled?
- How will you and your line manager know when you have achieved your role and your personal objectives? …

...

- When will you and your line manager meet to review your learning from this programme? (You must set four specific review dates over a six-month period following the programme in order to be accepted for a place.)

I've discussed my idea with the directors and the other senior managers. They've been very supportive because they see this as a way of ensuring that learning is taking place and that their investment in training (which I have to say is very high) is being wisely spent.

I'll let you know how well this idea works.

Keep in touch.

Jackie

From:	sara@e-mail.com
To:	jackie@e-mail.com
Sent:	30 September
Subject:	Action planning

Jackie

I wanted to let you know how the action planning is going.

I read your e-mail with interest and decided to steal the whole idea!

I would be interested to know how the process is working for you because I've had a huge variety of responses. When I discussed the plans with the senior managers they took a bit of convincing because all they could focus on was that their line managers would be doing an awful lot more work this way. I convinced them to try it by pointing out that if the learning was being implemented, then the staff would be taking more responsibility for their actions and therefore the line managers would have more time to manage. This seemed to hit the right note as for the past nine months we've really been trying to get managers to devolve responsibility right down the line.

So, having convinced the senior managers, I went to work on the line managers. Some of them truly welcomed the idea; they saw it as an opportunity to really get involved with the development of their staff. Others saw it as the training department wanting to get out of running courses! Eventually, after lots of one-to-one meetings, I had a majority of managers willing to go with the plans. The other managers are now following suit because I'm sticking to my guns and not accepting course nominations without fully completed action plans. I've been really lucky in this respect because my personnel director is backing me up 100 per cent.

I know it's early days, but now I'm really finding that when I start a course delegates are very focused on what they want to learn. This is making my life much more interesting – the delegates are more demanding and I have to be on my toes all the time. Also the demand for one-to-one coaching has gone up and I'm about to launch a mentoring scheme in order to meet this demand.

I find it truly amazing that one idea can lead to so much. Let me know what your experience is as soon as you can.

Sara

From:	jackie@e-mail.com
To:	sara@e-mail.com
Sent:	1 October
Subject:	Action planning

Sara

Glad to hear about the action planning working for you.

I've had a somewhat slower start and I'm pleased to hear that you think my idea was a good one.

I've implemented the action plans, but it seems that most line managers are against the idea at the moment. The senior management team has also backtracked and I've been told that I must go ahead with programmes where delegates have not presented action plans. This has been pretty frustrating, I can tell you.

Having said this, where the action plans are being used, the managers are being very good at following up and anecdotal evidence is suggesting that they're getting really good results. Now I'm planning to produce a report (brief, snappy, and interesting) to be circulated in various formats throughout the company, giving details of how the action plans work and why they're useful.

I am hoping that this softly, softly approach will start to bring a few more people on board.

Anyway, keep up the good work and I'll be in touch again very soon.

Jackie

Action points:
Summaries and
checklists

We hope you've enjoyed reading about our experiences and will find them helpful when dealing with your own problem issues.

This section summarizes our general thoughts about the various topics discussed in the e-mails and provides useful checklists and a sample training needs analysis form.

Clarifying training needs

Handling disagreements

Probably the hardest part of the training cycle is identifying the true training need. Very often people are sent on training events chosen by their line manager and therefore the success of the training depends upon the manager having chosen wisely.

On other occasions a person will ask to go on a course because he or she likes the sound of it and the manager will agree to it to keep the employee quiet. Often it's the people who shout the loudest who get the training – and the people who shout the loudest are the keen, enthusiastic ones who would probably learn anyway!

Over the years we've seen many people who are on the wrong course – some only there because they were sent, some who do not really need the training. As trainers we now believe that we only have two options for ways to deal with this: we can carry on regardless or we can confront the issue.

Carrying on regardless may seem like the easy option, but if the training department takes it too often credibility will be lost and trainers will be faced with increasing criticism that their training is not relevant or useful. We would therefore recommend finding a way to confront the issue (as in e-mail 21) and following this process:

- Do not train until you have completed some form of needs analysis (see below for methods).
- Always issue a pre-course questionnaire to all delegates, asking them to consider their personal objectives for the training. We recommend that this is discussed with, and signed off by, the delegate's line manager.
- Dedicate time to reading the pre-course questionnaires and consider amending your training to respond to the comments you receive.
- We also recommend that the objectives and outline for the training are signed off by the person who has commissioned the training – this

will ensure that no one comes back to you saying 'That's not what I asked for'.

- If someone on the course shows that they do not need the training, be prepared to discuss this with the delegate and his or her line manager.
- Spend time at the start of the course identifying personal objectives, experience levels and what people want to gain from the training experience.

Methods of training needs analysis

The following is a list of the different methods of training needs analysis we've tried. The list is not exhaustive, but it will give you some methods to consider:

- Questionnaires. A well-structured questionnaire will give you good information fairly quickly (so long as it is completed fully and honestly). Ask questions about the delegate's future role, skills, knowledge and behaviour requirements, about strengths and weaknesses and about problems that have occurred. Wherever possible, use a pilot for your questionnaire – this enables you to consider whether you're getting the type of answers you were looking for and, if not, will allow you to revise the questionnaire prior to full circulation.
- Interviews (structured and unstructured). In a structured interview individuals are asked a set list of questions, from which there is little deviation. This takes less time to conduct and analyse than an unstructured interview. However, an unstructured interview can lead to issues being uncovered that would not otherwise have come to light, purely because the conversation has flowed in a certain direction and because individuals tend to relax and talk openly in an unstructured interview. Having said this, the information gained from this form of interview will take time to sift through and analyse.
- Critical incident analysis. In a nutshell, this is a process where significant events, whether negative or positive, are considered and (in a training needs analysis context) questions such as 'What learning came from this situation?' and 'What knowledge, skills or behaviours need to be in place in order to prevent (a negative) situation, or reproduce (a positive) situation?', have to be addressed.
- Testing and re-testing. For some tasks and jobs, regular testing can highlight training needs. This process can be extremely time consuming; however, it does reap rewards and provides sound evidence that

training is required. Testing is probably most appropriate in relation to skills and knowledge (eg with individuals involved in operating equipment, or having to know certain legislation).

- Performance appraisal. The appraisal discussion is often used as a forum for considering training needs. For this to be effective, the appraiser must ask questions other than 'What training courses would you like to attend in the coming year?'. Questions should focus on development, eg what new projects will the person be involved in and therefore what skills, knowledge and behaviours will they require? Alternatively, discussions could be around areas of concern, eg 'I have noticed that you seem to be unclear about our budgetary processes, can you tell me more about why you're unclear?'.

The following example of a training needs analysis questionnaire has been reproduced with the kind permission of European Financial Data Services (UK) Limited.

TRAINING NEEDS ANALYSIS 2000

NAME OF TEAM: **MANAGER'S NAME:**

NUMBER OF STAFF: **INTERVIEWED BY:**
(including managers)

PART A: REVIEW OF TRAINING DURING 1999

1.   What type of training have members of your team received during 1999?

SUBJECT	TYPE OF TRAINING (course, on-the job with colleague, on-the-job with trainer, distance learning, or college)	% ATTENDED TO DATE (% attended to date)	% REQUIREMENT IN TEAM (% requiring training in team)

2.   How has this training impacted the performance of your team? Explain why.

3.   Did you have training requirements that were not met?

PART B: FUTURE TRAINING NEEDS:

4.   What are your training needs for 2000 for both permanent and temporary staff?

SUBJECT/LEARNING NEED	TYPE OF TRAINING (course, on-the job with colleague, on-the-job with trainer, distance learning, or college)	NOS.	IMPORTANCE m = must have s = should have c = could have	URGENCY 1 = now 2 = 1st qtr 3 = 3–6 mths 4 = 6–12 mths

5.   What are your business priorities/key result areas for 2000?

6a.   What will be your maximum headcount?
When?

What will be your minimum headcount?
When?

6b.   Do you have any plans to restructure the department/team?
If yes, will there be any training needs as a result?

PART C: REVIEW OF SERVICE PROVIDED BY T&D

7a.   What do you think about the support you have had from the T&D
       department during 1999?

7b.   Is there any other support or service you would like from us?

7c.   What reports or information about training would you like?

Designing interventions

Working with others

Trainers are not the only people within an organization designing or delivering training. Many other people may decide to get involved, after all training 'is not rocket science'. When a non-professional trainer designs a training event its content is often good, but three things are usually missing:

- clear, measurable learning objectives;
- participative learning methods;
- evaluation techniques.

As the training and development specialists, it is our job to help others follow a systematic approach, but without becoming too much like an 'anorak' about the subject. It is our role to help non-professional trainers by giving support, feedback and the benefit of our experience, rather than criticize and imply that only trainers should train. In many of the e-mails we talk about the way to address issues through communication with others; how to 'stay on side', but also give difficult messages.

Much is written about communication and assertiveness techniques, such as transactional analysis and NLP. (See Further Reading and see Delivering training: handling people for a list of assertive principles.)

A systematic approach to training

To ensure that training is properly designed and implemented, we recommend the following systematic approach:

Clarify the needs

Ask: Why is the training necessary? What are the knowledge, skills, and attitudes that are required? (See the section above, about different methods of training needs analysis.) At this stage, you also need to identify any other requirements or limitations. Areas to consider are:

- When the training is required by.
- Which people form the target audience and what experience they have.
- Organizational culture.
- Where the training will be – think about available space and equipment.

- Any ideas from the sponsor about specific content or methods.
- What the participants have been or will be told about the training.

Write aims and objectives

Once needs and requirements are clearly identified, the next stage is to write aims and objectives. There are many different ways of writing objectives and many excuses for avoiding it! As objectives help you confirm the content, establish methods, and evaluate the course, we like to use the opening sentence of 'By the end of this course/event/ experience participants will be able to...'. This is followed by a series of bullet points each beginning with a verb. For example, by the end of this paragraph, readers will be able to:

- Explain a systematic approach to delivering effective training.
- Show how to write clear learning objectives.
- Discuss styles of writing session notes.

Select methods and write session notes

What will you do on the day? See below for specific information about using different training methods. It's a good idea to write out session notes in full, with some examples of the sort of responses you are looking for from the participants.

Implement methods to conduct the training

This means actually doing the course or facilitating the learning – and it should definitely be the fun part.

Evaluate the learning

Ask the following questions:

- How did the event go?
- Was the course well designed?
- Did you achieve what you set out to do?
- Did participants learn what they needed to? How do you know?

Training methods: choosing activities and exercises

There are no hard and fast rules about choosing activities and exercises to use in a training session. Use the following list of questions as a checklist when you are putting together your training session:

- What do I know about the delegates for the training? What are their backgrounds? What activities are they likely to respond to? What are their learning styles? Does anyone have a disability or special need? What are their normal working hours?
- Does my session plan include time for some input on theory, some activity, some reflection and some action planning? Do I change the nature of the methods on a regular basis? Does my plan allow for any flexibility if some activities overrun or if delegates do not respond as I had planned?
- What facilities do I have available to me? What space is available for syndicate group work? Is there a TV/video player/video camera available? Are the chairs and tables fixed or moveable?
- What budget am I working with in terms of time and money? Can I afford to hire or buy videos and pre-prepared materials? Do I have the time to undertake a large-scale activity?
- Is the session part of a programme or a stand-alone? What implications does this have for the methods that I am using – will delegates get bored if I use the same structure for every session?

Available training methods
Here is a list (but not an exhaustive list) of the training methods available to you:

- **Input** (also called straight talk, chalk-and-talk or lecture). This is probably the method we as trainers like least. However, delegates come to training courses with an expectation that the trainer is going to provide them with some information – and they will feel cheated if input is not provided. Try to keep your input to a minimum and wherever possible intersperse it with questions to the group and discussion around the issues raised.
- **Buzz groups/pairs.** Using these involves putting a question to the group and asking them to discuss it in pairs or small groups (with a maximum of three or four people). Delegates do not leave their seats, and have a very brief discussion, after which the trainer takes feedback in the whole group.
- **Syndicate groups.** When in-depth discussion is required or activities are given that require work in small groups, you will probably use a syndicate group. These groups tend to work away from the main group and then come back together at the end of the activity to compare thoughts and comments. Often you will ask the group to

select a representative to give feedback to the whole group, with or without flipchart or OHPs.

- **Discussion.** This method will be used in conjunction with some of the others in this list. Discussion can be structured or unstructured, you may wish to ask delegates to consider one single comment, a case study or a very structured series of questions. Discussion may take place in small groups, where the group controls their own time. Alternatively, trainer-led discussion may take place in the whole group.

- **Case studies.** Here groups are given a scenario, based on a real-life situation relating to the topic at hand, and are asked one or a series of questions relating to the scenario.

- **Role-play.** This is a very powerful tool when used effectively. You can also cause many delegates great stress and trauma at the very mention of the words. We will often describe role-play as 'practising the skills' to soften the impact. This method involves delegates in taking on a role, either as themselves or another person, and working through a situation as if the situation were occurring there and then. There are many different variations on role-play and we would recommend that you read around this subject and discuss it with others before embarking on using it.

- **In-tray exercise.** Delegates are put into a situation where they receive an 'in-tray' pack containing letters, e-mails, telephone messages, etc and they are asked to deal with them in ways relating to the training topic. The trainer can then add to the in-tray, changing priorities, providing more information and so on. In-tray exercises can be used very effectively in time management, project management, delegation, general supervisory skills and management development sessions.

- **Quizzes.** A quick quiz is a very effective way of testing how far delegates have progressed with their learning and can also be used to lift the energy within a group. Quizzes can take many formats – as paper-based quizzes, pub quizzes, TV/radio show rip-offs (be creative – you can adapt many shows in a training setting) and others.

- **'Activities'.** This is an all-encompassing term describing the various exercises that trainers use. For example, building towers, crossing imaginary rivers, blindfolded walks and parachute games. The list of possibilities is endless. Be creative, use your imagination, and don't be afraid to try something new.

When you are choosing a training method, our final rule is this: make sure that the method fits in with the objectives for the training and that it will enhance the learning that takes place.

Delivering training

Effective administration

Administration is probably one of the key roles within a training department or company and also one of the most underrated. It is concerned with the setting up and running of effective systems and procedures to support training activities. In some companies, the trainers do their own administration; in others, there is a dedicated administrator. Either way, the work that needs doing is the same. Here are some ideas about what administrative tasks are required to support training:

- Creating and maintaining training policy and strategy.
- Creating training calendars and/or timetables.
- Collating nominations for courses.
- Keeping course brochures and information.
- Booking training venues and equipment.
- Liaising with external training providers.
- Handling travel arrangements for trainers and participants.
- Booking staff on to training courses.
- Sending out joining instructions, pre- and post-course work.
- Confirming attendance on courses and events.
- Organizing refreshments and accommodation.
- Creating exercises, handouts and workbooks.
- Welcoming trainees to the training area.
- Co-ordinating expense claims and invoices.
- Monitoring follow-ups with line managers.
- Collating of evaluation forms.
- Sending out training certificates.
- Handling stationery requirements.
- Maintaining training records.
- Producing training reports for business and line managers.

See e-mail 8 for a checklist of what questions an administrator might want to ask when organizing a specific training event.

Handling people

All too often we don't discuss with someone the effect their behaviour is having due to our own limiting beliefs – the fears that someone will be upset, annoyed, unable to cope or will dislike us. There is also a temptation to fall into the compassion trap – thinking that others' needs have priority over one's own. As trainers we are concerned with learning, that is bringing about a change in someone's behaviour. Yet we often find ourselves torn between being nice to people and giving them the feedback they need in order to develop. Also, trainers often think that they have to be perfect, or the expert, and, therefore, if we find someone difficult, we feel it must be because of something we've done, rather than inappropriate behaviour from the other person. In order to handle these situations we need to overcome our limiting beliefs and negative internal messages.

While there are some specific techniques you can use for dealing with different types of people and their behaviours, you will notice from the e-mails that there are a number of common threads that form a strategy for handling people.

Reviewing your motives

When you are experiencing a problem with a trainee, before doing anything you need to be honest with yourself. What is the real issue and why are you finding it difficult? Is the issue really something that the trainee could do something about, or are you the problem? Behaviour breeds behaviour – so what are you reacting to? How important is addressing the issue to achieving the purpose of the training and maintaining group stability? What will you gain by addressing the issue, and who will benefit? What might you lose? What is your intention in addressing the situation? You need to balance your professional role with your personal feelings.

Preparing yourself

The only way you can successfully handle a problem with someone is to prepare yourself properly. We suggest that you think through, and maybe write down, what you want to say and how you are going to say it, as well as considering what the other person's reactions might be. Bear in mind two old expressions: 'Never judge another until you have walked for one week in their shoes' and 'Treat others as you would expect to be treated'. We also suggest that you practise what you're going to say, in the mirror, or with a friend.

Giving and accepting feedback

The e-mails suggest a three-stage approach to giving feedback. This works just as well for positive and negative feedback:

1. Tell the person what the issue is. Concentrate on performance and behaviour (what we do) rather than personality (what we are). Give specific examples that the person can link to the precise behaviour and circumstances.
2. Explain the result of the behaviour. For this you need to ask yourself: 'How did the behaviour affect the situation or people involved? What was the general effect? How did you feel or think?'.
3. State clearly what you would like to happen. Examples of this are: 'We can discuss why it happened'; 'I want you to continue doing this'; 'I want you to stop doing it'; 'I want to agree a way forward'.

Use the following as a checklist for giving feedback:

- Concentrate on the behaviour not on the person.
- Direct the feedback towards behaviour that the person can do something about.
- Be specific.
- Use observations, not inferences.
- Give feedback as soon as possible after an event.
- Be clear about your motives.
- Give positive as well as negative feedback (where appropriate).
- Don't overload a person with feedback.

Accepting feedback is as hard as giving it (and for some of us, it's harder). To help you really hear feedback from others:

- Listen.
- Check your understanding.
- Try not to be defensive.
- Ask for examples.
- Choose what to do with the feedback.

- Relate the feedback to other situations.
- Check the feedback with others.

Communication techniques

As trainers it is vital that we consider how different people hear different messages, and how best to communicate with others. Communication techniques can be helped by using the following assertive principles:

- Try to maintain an open channel of communication between you and the other person.
- Expressions, eye contact and other mannerisms should be consistent with what you are saying so that you look and sound genuine.
- Be ready for a working compromise: at least be prepared to listen to the other person and recognize that he or she may not share your point of view. Consider the possibility of changing your own position and viewpoint.
- Ask for what you want or need, clearly and directly.
- When people are being aggressive, manipulative or just rude to you, try not to take it personally. Deal with people without feeling that you have to make them like you or approve of you.
- Show you understand the other person's point of view, perhaps by echoing part of his or her last sentence, or saying something like, 'Yes, I see what you mean' or 'From what you say, it's obvious to me that you disagree'.
- Try to be confident enough to state your point of view and opinions. You will almost certainly gain in confidence by expressing your opinions and values.
- Avoid judging the other person.
- Take responsibility for your mistakes.
- Beware of limiting benefits – often we do not do or say something because we fear what others will do or say. If you give your message assertively, as set out in this checklist, your views will probably be taken seriously.
- Keep working on the 'relationship' – the mutual respect that exists between the two people communicating. Adopting an assertive approach should ensure that you are able to remain honest and genuine when talking to each other.

Evaluating learning

Validation and evaluation

Evaluation is a vast topic and one that always causes debate amongst trainers. We are usually very good at presenting reaction sheets (or 'happy sheets') at the end of a course. But how can we be sure that the training we have delivered has a) met its objectives and b) been of benefit to the delegates and the organization? Here are some of our thoughts on evaluation, presented according to the five-levels theory suggested by D L Kirkpatrick:

- Level one – reaction
  - Reaction sheets. Your reaction sheets (often referred to as 'happy sheets') should ask questions about the achievement of the course objectives, about the course material, the presentation, the activities used, the venue and the pre-course material.
  - Group discussion. Build in time at the end of the course for delegates to work in small groups to discuss their reaction to the day and how they will take the learning forward. Have them record the main points of the discussion for you to take away.
  - Thumbs up, thumbs down. This is *very* focused on reaction. Ask closed questions about the training course directed to the whole group. If participants feel the answer to the question is 'Yes', they give a thumbs-up sign, if the answer is 'No', it's a thumbs down. You need to record the number of responses, positive or negative, to each question.

- Level two – learning
  - Reaction sheets. Questions about what participants feel they have learnt during the course can be included on the reaction sheets.
  - Post-course review. Delegates should meet with their line manager soon after the course to discuss what learning has taken place and how this will be applied. They should then meet at agreed intervals to review how much progress is being made.
  - Action plans. By requiring delegates to complete action plans at the end of a course, we imply that we are expecting them to implement some learning from the course and make some changes in the way they work.

- Level three – effects on individual performance
  - Post-course review with line manager, (as described in level two).
  - Follow-up questionnaire. The trainer circulates a questionnaire to all delegates and their managers asking questions about how the learning from the course is being applied.
  - Follow-up calls. The trainer, or a nominated person, chooses a random sample of delegates from a course and then contacts them and their line managers to ask a series of questions about the application of learning from the course.
  - Re-testing. If the training is very skills-based and has culminated with a test, it is possible (although time-consuming) to re-test delegates on a regular basis and then to retrain if necessary.

- Level four – effects on team performance
  In order to measure effects of training on team performance there must be some measure of training need prior to the training taking place. Examples of measurements are:

  - customer complaints;
  - error rates;
  - work outstanding;
  - tasks completed per hour/day/week;
  - self-assessment of performance by team members.

  Once such measurements have been recorded, the training can be carried out and new measurements completed at intervals following the training.

- Level five – effects on organizational performance
  As with level three evaluation, in order to assess the effects of training on an organization, measures need to be taken prior to the training being carried out. Examples of such measures are:

  - staff attitude surveys;
  - profit levels;
  - wastage;
  - levels of consumables used;
  - accidents and damage rates;
  - customer complaints;
  - working rates.

As with level three evaluation, measures will need to be taken periodically following the training.

Obviously, at levels three, four and five other factors come into play and success obviously cannot be attributed solely to training. However, if training is one of the activities that has taken place, some change must be related to this.

Further reading

van Adelsberg, D and Trolley, E (1999) *Running Training Like a Business*, The Forum Group – Berett Koehler, San Francisco

Back, K and K (1992) *Assertiveness at Work*, McGraw-Hill (PLACE)

Bee F and R, (1994) *Training Needs Analysis and Evaluation*, Institute of Personnel and Development, London

Bond, T (1990) *Games for Social and Life Skills*, Stanley Thornes, (London)

Bourner, T, Martin, V and Race, P (1993) *Workshops that Work: 100 ideas to make your training events more effective*, (Training Series), McGraw-Hill, London

Bramley, P (1991) *Evaluating Training Effectiveness*, McGraw-Hill, London

Cava, R (1990) *Dealing with Difficult People*, Piatkus Books, London

Christopher, E and Smith, L (1993) *Leadership Training Through Gaming* Kogan Page, London

Diane Bailey Associates ed. *The Training Handbook*, GEE Publishing Ltd, London

Goleman, D (1996) *Emotional Intelligence*, Bloomsbury Publishing, London

Hardingham, A (1998) *Psychology for Trainers*, IPD, London

Hay, J (1993) *Working it Out at Work: Understanding attitudes and building relationships*, Sherwood Publishing, Watford

Honey, P and Mumford, A (1986) *A Manual of Learning Styles*, Honey, London

Hurst, B (1991) *The Handbook of Communication Skills*, Kogan Page, London

O'Connor, J and Seymour, J (1994) *Training with NLP*, Thorsons, San Francisco

Pont, T (1991) *Developing Effective Training Skills*, McGraw-Hill, (London)

Reece, I and Walker, S (1994) *A Practical Guide to Teaching, Training and Learning*, Business Education Publishers, (Great Britain)

(Authors: various) (1997) *Making Training Pay*, IPD, London

Ready Made Activities – Developing your Staff Resource Pack, The Institute of Management/Pitman Publishing, London

(Authors: various) 1996 *Inside Out – values and attitudes training for those involved in personal development*, The Guide Association, London

Glossary

Training has a language all of its own. The following terms are used throughout the book and these definitions outline our understanding of them. Words in italics in the glossary definitions also have their own main entry.

Activist   one who learns through doing and prefers activity-based training. The activist *learning style* is one of four *learning styles* identified by Honey and Mumford.

Activity   any event, large or small, designed to promote *learning*. An activity requires participation from an individual or group. An activity may also be referred to as an exercise, a task or a game.

Aim   the overall statement of intent from the *trainer*. It describes what the *trainer* is hoping to achieve during the programme and is informed by the identified needs.

Analysis   the examination of various aspects of a situation to find out what is at the bottom of it. When we analyse we ask questions such as 'What is happening here? Why is this happening? What needs to happen in order to improve the situation?'.

Assertiveness   a *skill*; a way of behaving and communicating that draws on our rational, adult side. When we are communicating assertively we are able to put our point across, whilst respecting that other people have valid points to make. The concept that underpins assertiveness is that everybody has a certain set of rights which can be asserted.

Assessment   a general term describing a set of methods used to ascertain the effectiveness of *training* and *learning*.

Attitudes   the ways in which people act out their feelings or opinions. Attitudes are formed throughout life and changing them is one of the challenges for *trainers*. Attitudes are displayed by the way in which people behave (their *behaviours*) and therefore by changing *behaviour* we can start working towards changing attitudes.

Behaviour   the way in which people do things. Changing trainees' behaviour is one of the most challenging and exciting areas of *training*. In *training* we often concentrate on *knowledge* and *skills* since changes in these areas are often easy to measure. However, the ways in which people implement *knowledge* and *skills* are just as important.

CPD   Continuing Professional Development – a term that is now used very widely. It describes the fact that everyone should be *learning* all the time and that we should find ways of identifying and recording our *learning*.

Delegate   an individual who is participating in a *training* event. Delegates may also be called trainees or *participants*.
Development   a continuous process of growing and *learning*. By developing we continuously become more than we were.

Evaluation   a term used in many different ways by *trainers*. We view evaluation as the monitoring of the overall effectiveness of a *training programme*. This involves analysing how the *training* has been of value to the individual, the team and the organization, not simply whether the *training* has achieved the stated *objectives*. We also believe evaluation should include some measure of monetary value. Thorough evaluation of *training* is often difficult.

Feedback   a word with two meanings in this book. When used relating to a *training session* it describes the way comments are taken from the whole group (*plenary group*) after *syndicate group* work or after an *activity*. In the broader context, the term feedback is used to describe constructive comment about actions, situations or issues.

Ground rules   guidelines for ways of working in a *training session*. Ground rules should be agreed with a training group at the start of the session. They may include statements relating to equal opportunities, expectations in terms of *behaviour* and also practical details such as starting and finishing on time.

Intervention   a course, self-study period or any similar experience, carried out in order to cause change. A *training* or *learning* intervention involves helping participants develop new *skills*, *attitudes* or *behaviour* to help them respond more effectively in a given situation.

Knowledge   the ability to recall information about a situation or issue. Knowledge incorporates facts, figures, methods, processes and ideas.

Learner   any person who is participating in a *learning* experience.

Learning   the process of increasing *knowledge* and *skills*, and developing our *attitudes* or beliefs, so that we have the opportunity for increased choice. When we learn something new, we can choose whether or not to adopt it in our daily work.

Learning experience   anything from which a person learns – it may be a *training session*, but it could equally be the experience of shadowing a colleague, reading articles or books or dealing with a difficult customer.

Learning styles   the ways in which individuals prefer to learn. Honey and Mumford's research identified four general learning styles: *activist*, *reflector*, *theorist*, and *pragmatist*.

Module   a part of a series forming a 'modular programme' – each module in the programme will stand alone, but will fit in to a wider *learning* strategy. In an effective programme, the *learning* from each module builds upon the *learning* from the previous module.

Objective   a specific statement of something that a trainee will be able to do at the end of a period of *learning*.

Participant   anyone participating in a *training event*. We also use the words *delegate* or trainee, but we are more likely to use *delegate* if we are talking about a training course, whereas participant could describe a person taking part in any *learning* experience.

Participative   describes any process during which individuals are required to take part in some type of *activity*.

Plenary group   the whole training group. We often talk about taking *feedback* in plenary: this means coming back together as a whole group for a discussion.

Pragmatist   one who learns effectively when able to apply the *learning* to their own situation. A pragmatist prefers practicality to theory. The pragmatist *learning style* is one of the four *learning styles* identified by Honey and Mumford.

Reflection   a *learning* tool. When we reflect we consider what has gone on in the past and what we have learnt or can learn. The past may be the immediate past such as an *activity* just undertaken or it may be more distant.

Reflector   a person who enjoys learning from *reflection*. The reflector *learning style* is one of the four *learning styles* identified by Honey and Mumford.

Skills   something that an individual is able to do. Skills tend to involve some sort of physical application of *knowledge*. The *knowledge* may be on a conscious or an unconscious level. When we are *learning* a skill we go through a four-stage process:

1. Unconscious incompetence (I don't know that I don't know).
2. Conscious incompetence (I know that I don't know).
3. Conscious competence (I know that I know).
4. Unconscious competence (I don't know that I know).

When we forget that we ever needed to learn many basic skills such as walking, eating and dressing it is because we have reached unconscious competence. Part of a trainer's role is to help people 'unpick' their unconscious competence in order to improve their performance in certain areas.

Syndicate group   a small group forming part of the whole training group, also referred to as a breakout group.

Theorist   one who likes to know the theories behind a piece of *learning* or the ideas that back up comments being made. The theorist *learning style* is one of the four *learning styles* identified by Honey and Mumford.

Trainer   a person who is helping others to learn.

Training   a systematic process by which an individual learns *skills*, *knowledge* and *behaviour* that are required in order to respond to a specific situation, to do a job or fulfil a particular role.

Training course   a group of people coming together with the specific intention of learning certain *skills*, *knowledge* and *behaviour* in order to fulfil specific objectives.

Training event   any structured event where *training* is taking place. This could be a workshop, a *training course* or a *training programme*.

Training need   an identified gap in an individual's *skills*, *knowledge* or *behaviour*, which prevents the individual from performing effectively.

Training programme a chronological outline of a series of activities that take place in order to achieve a set of stated *objectives*. On occasion we may use the term training programme interchangeably with *training event* or *training course*.

Training session a part of a *training programme* – it is a single event that forms part of a whole. A *training course* or *training programme* may comprise a series of different training sessions.

Understanding the ability to consider a concept and relate that concept to individual *knowledge* and experience. With understanding, I am able to apply my considerations in a variety of situations and I am able to draw logical conclusions by processing information relating to the concept.

Validation use of a variety of methods to find out whether a *training course* has achieved its *objectives*, and whether the *participants* have learnt what the trainer wanted them to.

Values the concepts that underpin our *attitudes* and therefore our *behaviours*. Values are deep-rooted beliefs, the things that motivate us and drive us forward.

Visual aids anything that can be seen and that will help to enhance the *learning* taking place during a *training session*. *Trainers* must ensure that visual aids are of good quality and that they will enhance sessions rather than distract *delegates*.

Workshop a type of *training session*. During a workshop, *delegates* can expect to take part in a variety of *activities* in order to help them learn. The nature of workshops is that they are very *participative*.

Index